THE **BRAIN** SUTRAS

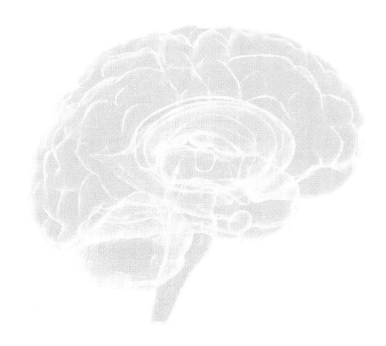

A. Martin Wuttke

Copyright ©2019

I salute the supreme teacher,
the truth, whose nature is bliss;
who is the giver of the highest happiness;
who is pure wisdom;
who is beyond all qualities and infinite like the sky;
who is beyond words;
who is one and eternal, pure and still;
who is beyond all change and phenomena
and who is the silent witness to all our thoughts and emotions –
I salute truth, the supreme teacher.

(ANCIENT VEDIC HYMN)

This book is dedicated to Roy Eugene Davis and the lineage of Kriya Yoga teachers.

Contents

Brain Sutra 1
The Psycho-physiological Correlates of Spiritual Transformation 01

Brain Sutra 2
Consciousness Is Modified by the Condition of the Brain 03

Brain Sutra 3
The Brain Is the Organ of the Mind 05

Brain Sutra 4
The Observer Is Not Separate from the Object Being Observed 08

Brain Sutra 5
The Nature of One's Spiritual Practice 10

Brain Sutra 6
You Are the Entire Ocean 13

Brain Sutra 7
Real Healing Is Spiritual 15

Brain Sutra 8
The Big Picture: A Perspective on the Evolution of Ourselves and Humanity ... 20

Brain Sutra 9
Have You Had a Wake-up Call? 25

Brain Sutra 10
Have You Had a Wake-up Call? 33

Brain Sutra 11 – Part 1
Navigating Through theLayers of the Mind 40

Brain Sutra 11 – Part 2
  Clearing the Subconscious 47

Brain Sutra 12
  Truth 53

Brain Sutra 13
  The Origin and the Science of Superconscious Meditation 56

Brain Sutra 14
  Get into the Gap 63

Brain Sutra 15
  A Continuation of Sutra 14, "Get into the Gap" 70

Brain Sutra 16
  Merging Science and Mysticism 76

Brain Sutra 17
  Making It Real 81

Brain Sutra 18
  Think in the Gap 85

Brain Sutra 19
  Our Natural State 89

Brain Sutra 20
  Nature or Nurture? 94

Brain Sutra 21
  Our Bodies Are Keeping Score 97

Brain Sutra 22
  The Inner Light and the God Spot 106

Brain Sutra 23
  The Truth Is Simple 110

Brain Sutra 24
  The Experience of the Inner Light and the Inner Sound 112

Brain Sutra 25
  "Liberation for Oneself and Service to Mankind." 120

Brain Sutra 1

The Psycho-physiological Correlates of Spiritual Transformation

As units of pure consciousness we express through the brain and nervous system.

At the innermost core we are clear, immortal being without conditioning. The body and mind serve as a vehicle for the Soul and, as such, pure consciousness in the unaware state is conditioned by impressions that accumulate and are inherent in the body/mind. As a result we are forgetful of our true identity as the Self or eternal witness.

This primal awareness, the life of our life, is always subtly present in the background. In this sense awareness is always the same; you have the same awareness now that you had as a child, just different thoughts/ideas/beliefs accumulated and scattered about the different levels of mind. Nevertheless, awareness remains the same—ever pure, witnessing. The goal of spiritual practice is to return to, and consciously experience, this pure awareness.

> Our birth is but a sleep and a forgetting:
> The Soul that rises with us, our life's Star,
> Hath had elsewhere its setting,
> And cometh from afar:
> Not in entire forgetfulness,
> And not in utter nakedness,

> But trailing clouds of glory do we come
> From God, who is our home:
> Heaven lies about us in our infancy!
>
> —William Wordsworth

Note: The words Divine Being, Supreme Being, consciousness, truth, God, absolute, Source, ultimate Reality, essence *or* core of our Being, *all refer to the same thing and are used interchangeably throughout these sutras.*

Brain Sutra 2

Consciousness Is Modified by the Condition of the Brain

Consciousness is modified by the condition, and the conditionings, of the brain.

The brain is shaped by the effects of our genetic, biological, environmental, and karmic influences. Indeed, it is malleable—a concept known as neuroplasticity.

Genetics will govern our inherited physical characteristics, sex, and even our predisposition for certain behavior. There are specific polymorphisms (genetic mutations) that, in combination, will affect brain chemistry (neurotransmitters and neurohormones). This can have a strong influence on our stress tolerance and ultimately on emotional and physical health. However, not all genetic markers are destined to manifest. Many are dormant and triggered by stress from other sources. Biological and environmental exposure will also have direct effects on brain development.

Karmic influences, as cause and effect mechanisms, are set in motion and will also have direct effects on the networks set down in the brain.

A nurturing, calm, healthy, socialized environment will create pathways in the brain conducive to higher resiliency and balanced brain/body chemistry.

The brain-mind is the vehicle of consciousness. Depending on the health of the brain and the psychological impressions and conditionings, consciousness is more or less clouded.

Consciousness is pure when unmodified—just simply aware of being aware. It is the light or life we call "I" that is silently witnessing all that we experience.

Brain Sutra 3

—⚭—

The Brain Is the Organ of the Mind

The brain is the organ of the mind and therefore the health and condition of the brain has effects on the expression of consciousness through the mind.

If the brain is not performing optimally, then the expression of consciousness will be hindered as clouds hide the sun.

If our goal is to be a clear conduit for our Divine nature, then there are some practical things we can do to achieve the highest physical and psychological function.

Eat well. The food and drink we take in has enormous impact on brain chemistry. Food should be pure and as "alive" as possible. Heavy, dead, overprocessed food will dull the mind and limit our attempts to concentrate, meditate, and quiet the mind. However, becoming too concerned with the body and diet can be a distraction.

Move your body. Exercise is essential to optimal brain function. Research identifies exercise as a critical factor in keeping the brain healthy and holding off Alzheimer's disease. There is evidence that exercising in short intervals throughout the day is much more beneficial than going to the gym an hour a day.

Observe your thoughts. Psychological/emotional trauma during crucial developmental periods affects the pathways in the brain. Negative ramifications throughout one's life resulting from developmental trauma often conceal the causal event or events that produced the conditioning.

This is often why we react to negative circumstances, or to people, in habitual patterns. However, before we can clear out these negative patterns and conditionings, we must first stop unconsciously reinforcing negative patterns. This requires us to sharpen our ability to observe ourselves and to be vigilant in regard to triggers and to the impressions we allow into our minds.

Be aware of your environment. Neuroscience researchers recently discovered that our environment has a continual modifying effect on our brains. In other words, the messages we receive from media, friends, family, and authority shape our brain pathways. We can counter this by only allowing information from conscious and enlightened sources. We can consciously nourish our minds with positive impressions. Natural environments, as well as classical music, art, and great literature produced by enlightened minds has a nourishing effect upon the Soul.

When the body and mind are tired or stressed it is wise to avoid some of the contemporary mass-media influences, as we are more likely to have our guard down in these states.

Create a sacred space in your life. A practical thing we can do is to create a space and, if possible, a room that we can devote to daily meditation and inspirational reading. Devotional items in the room such as flowers, candles, and pictures of saints and teachers can create an uplifting environment. The space should be used only for purposes of meditation, prayer, and contemplation. In this way the brain will find a respite from stress, and the space will become a retreat, conducive in itself as uplifting and restorative to our Soul.

Brain Sutra 4

The Observer Is Not Separate from the Object Being Observed

The mind, when unaware of its true nature and its origin, perceives, translates, defines, and relates to the objects of consciousness incorrectly as the "external world."

The mystic understands there is only one universal mind containing all knowledge—complete and whole. We are like travelers experiencing different levels of it as we evolve.

> You are the universe expressing itself as a human for a little while.
>
> ECKHART TOLLE

The universe is an extension of Being, and although everything appears to be external to us, in Reality, matter or substance is simply consciousness in various stages of taking form. Physicists know that matter is just energy, frequencies or vibrations. Yogic science defines matter as consciousness—one thing expressing as…

The seer, seeing, and that which is seen are one.

The brain must be functioning optimally in order for perception to be refined to the state where this inner vision can be unveiled. This unveiling process requires the gradual transformation of the brain and nervous system, including removal of the incorrect thoughts or misperceptions that are influential. The instinctive nature must be purified and the intellectual mind must be seen for what it is: a tool.

The mind creates the world by the impressions that have been consciously and unconsciously stored. Definitions, interpretations, and judgments are essentially "learned." One must start with the truth about the world around us, moving toward resisting and transforming our faulty perceptions. This can be cultivated by a meditation practice that ultimately will lead to the awakening of spiritual insight/intuition.

If one sees God, the absolute, divine Being flowing through and as all things—there is nothing else. This is the real nature of Reality; if we do not live in this awareness it is only our misperception that keeps us from seeing this.

Do this:

A well-known spiritual teacher, Joel Goldsmith, gave his students a final task at the conclusion of his last public lecture, "Meditation on the Presence," in London on June 15, 1964. He made his conscious transition less than forty-eight hours later.

Paraphrased: Every day look at (at least) one person (it does not matter who—friend, enemy, stranger) and do not look at the outside, the form, the vehicle, the "human" identity; especially do not listen to your human interpretations if you have them. Look through that person's eyes to the life force that is animating them...to the pure divine Being. Do this silently, secretly, and sacredly...and realize that they, and everyone, and everything you see is That. Do this, make it a daily practice, a spiritual path, and then you will see what happens...because when you acknowledge this divine Presence in the world, the world can only reflect that knowing back to you.

Brain Sutra 5

—ɷ—

The Nature of One's Spiritual Practice

The spiritual path is very easy for one who gives first preference to it, who gives it supremacy over all other things. A differentiation of mild, middle, and intense natures also exists.
Patanjali Yoga Sutras 21, 22

Are you mild, in the middle, or of the intense nature on your path?

Mild: One who is curious about but not really committed to self-evolution. There is a tendency to have a lot of doubts and judgments. This type will go from teacher to teacher, seminar to seminar, searching but always maintaining some distance and never quite willing (or simply do not recognize the need) to put in the sincere effort it takes to begin (and engage in) the awakening process.

Middle: One who has found a teaching but still puts it in second place to all priorities in life. This type recognizes the need for a personal program of self-discipline, but is not yet able to embrace this truth as a personal realization. It remains more of an obligation often motivated from the perspective "This is what I should be doing."

Intense: One who fully recognizes the meaning and purpose of life: that we are here to awaken to our Divine nature. Therefore, one arranges one's life around one's spiritual path rather than trying to fit time in for spiritual pursuits. At this level one is a "disciple"—root of the word *discipline*.

A disciple is one who engages in a systematic program of action whose conscious intent is to achieve complete awakening and Self-realization. The spiritual practices and disciplines eventually lead to the awareness that one's entire life, everything one does—profession, relationships, and community—*is* the spiritual path.

There are people who have no interest whatsoever in spiritual matters, and this is fine, too. Every Soul will eventually wake up to the truth of their Being.

No matter where we find ourselves on the path, growth is facilitated and accelerated when we make a commitment to:

1. Practice superconscious meditation every day.
2. Study sources of inspirational higher knowledge.
3. Have fun! Enjoy life! But avoid being exposed to too much sensational, superficial, and useless information.
4. Practice being conscious, practical, honest, generous, compassionate, and appropriate in everything you do. See yourself, everyone, and everything as having its source in divine Being. (This is the most important spiritual practice we can engage in.)

If you haven't yet found a teacher or teaching you feel comfortable with, be patient, open your heart. With faith, know that the right and appropriate information, people and circumstances will unfold in a Divine order—the universe is intelligence itself and provides all we need according to our ability to accept it—this is being open to the flow of Grace. Doors open, often unexpectedly, when we are ready; this is a law of the universe.

So what is an intense level of practice? This could be perceived as a practice that is led by being clearly and continuously focused on the goals of "waking up," where the student sees all aspects of their life as an opportunity for spiritual growth. The more that practice is incorporated into daily life, permeating all action, the sooner the veil of Maya (ignorance, illusion) diminishes. But here our Western conditioning may tend to push too hard, so caution needs to be exercised when our egos urge us to "do more, work more, be more!" This caution reminds us that any practice or lifestyle that pushes on, disregarding balance and harmony will generally lead to lopsided development, and an outlook that is too rigid. By keeping these thoughts in mind, we are less likely to become attached to our practice and much less likely to judge and define ourselves by our progress (or lack thereof), which means we'll be less likely to be distracted from our true goal. The bottom line is, all practice should be balanced by non-attachment.

RAE INDIGO TEACHER TRAINING

Brain Sutra 6

—〰—

You Are the Entire Ocean

Rather than seeing Reality as it is, the ordinary mind perceives Reality from an illusory perspective. You are not a body producing consciousness, you are consciousness producing a body.

Self-Realized individuals see the world as a play of light as if projected on a screen. Good and evil, light and dark, "us" versus "them," are all manifestations of one thing, one divine Presence; there simply is not anything else, because this Presence creates, upholds, and imbues *all* that exists.

This is not an intellectual understanding to which only scientists studying quantum field mechanics are privy. It cannot be sufficiently conveyed or described with words… It cannot be known with the mind or intellect. It can only be experienced: a real experience relative to the superconscious state, which is the Soul's awareness when it is unencumbered. This may seem beyond our understanding. However, this perception is a potential every individual has within them—each one of us is an expression of the divine Source (divine Consciousness). This Consciousness *is* the life force; it is more evident in animate creatures but is fully present as what appears inanimate as well.

The mind, in its ordinary state, sees separation where there is wholeness. We are part of a connected, living, flowing universe. Everyone has a unique role to play in the unfolding of life.

> You are not a drop in the ocean.
> You are the entire ocean in a drop.
>
> — RUMI

Eventually every Soul, without exception, is destined to awaken to full Self-realization.

There are many who simply do not grasp, know about, or believe the possibility. There are many who do not know that Self-realization, and what it reveals, even exists. Throughout the millennia, enlightenment teaching traditions have given us tools and told us it is possible to transform one's own consciousness so that the accurate and true perception is unveiled. This is the purpose of a spiritual path. We can engage in a process of spiritual practice with faith that our efforts will bring about transformation.

Neuroscience is now confirming the brain changes that occur with spiritual practice.

Know that the same life that *is* you, that is your breath, that senses the world within and without, enables you to move, think, feel, and know that you are "you"... is the same life, the same silent divine Presence, that is everyone and everything.

When we consciously acknowledge this, our being is transformed; we open a new level of possibilities and profound perception. This is healing at the deepest level—this is truth consciousness.

Brain Sutra 7

—⚍—

Real Healing Is Spiritual

It is permanent and removes all doubt and fear. It is a realization of the Soul.

What is spiritual healing?

In regard to our work, I am often asked, "What makes what you do different?"

For over thirty years I have attempted to be as scientifically congruent as possible, to utilize the latest cutting-edge technology and to integrate the spiritual awareness and knowledge I have received from my personal practice and, most profoundly, the knowledge that has been transmitted to me from my guru.

Neurofeedback equipment, protocols, and science has the effect of holding a mirror up to a client's brain and consciousness, opening up the healing resources within him or her. However, there is another factor at work in what I do.

Technology is not what makes what we do different—technology is secondary.

Many clinicians are using neurofeedback with a high degree of success. Technology is able to give feedback that is displayed as a translation of the electrical dance (brain waves) of the brain cells. It is extraordinary how through technology one can give clients access to subtle levels of their own being—making them conscious of it. This is why neurofeedback is remarkably successful. Although we use this amazing technology in our work, what makes us different has come from realization, nothing else. This is *the most* important factor and is paramount to our results, training, and teaching.

But first we have to distinguish two types of healing.

1. Instinctive/physical. This is aimed primarily at the body, including physiology and subtle energy. There are many healing modalities for this, and most of us are, of course, very concerned with the health and maintenance of these bodies we (temporarily) inhabit. Of course the mind and emotions are involved, but the majority of "instinctive" approaches tend to operate in the realm of "duality," and we must be careful not to overly identify with our bodies and get too fixated on them.

   This level of healing is very important and useful, but we are looking beyond that—and this has far-reaching implications.

   And that is...

2. Spiritual healing. Spiritual healing comes about through the progressively deeper and more profound realization of Truth principles and can be cultivated through the following:

a. Heal yourself first by unfolding your higher understanding through dedicated spiritual practice.

b. Learn to look through the appearances: no one is "special" and yet everyone is special. We all have unique personality characteristics, but this is not "who" we really are and no individual is more or less special than anyone else—everyone is Divinity expressing itself. These "personalities" are temporary and illusory identities. Therefore we look impartially through the problem and personality and look beyond duality (good vs. bad, right vs. wrong), and acknowledge the Truth for ourselves and for those who come to us for healing.

This truth is: there is only one consciousness playing all the roles, manifesting as all that is: Divine Intelligence—omnipresent, omniscient, and omnipotent.

The healer/clinician's knowledge of this truth resonates with the deepest level of the client's being. And no matter if the client recognizes it or not, is aware of it or not, this will bring forth a corresponding resonant response from within the Soul of the client. This is an acknowledgment and recognition of Divinity and occurs silently, secretly, and sacredly. This is why being in the presence (which is a palpable invisible "field") of a spiritual master—someone who has realized the Truth (one who is Self- and God-realized), will have a spiritually uplifting and quickening effect.

At first, learning to see people and things this way is an intellectual exercise, a daily practice we undertake. We encounter difficulty training our minds to stop personalizing, judging, analyzing and/or projecting our own subconscious beliefs and conditionings upon the people who come to us. The way to overcome this is through item number 1 above: have a dedicated spiritual practice.

Eventually, spiritual practice will lead us beyond intellectual understanding to realization. Realization often first occurs as spontaneous moments of experience and "aha's" where we begin to sense the interconnectedness of everything. With time, realization reveals the highest truths and becomes permanent: we are no longer fooled by the illusion of separateness, of "you and me," "us and them." Rather we behold everyone and everything as a manifestation of Divinity.

When we have this level of realization, everything and everyone in our "field" is affected by this, again because of the resonant effect.

However, as we approach full Self-realization, we will see that along the way our realization is not yet fully complete, because we have moments of forgetting; moments where our human-ness and conditionings are dominant; our behaviors and reactions are not always conscious or as we would like them to be. As long as we are sincere and diligent in our efforts and our intention to know the Truth, our Soul's knowing will still radiate forth and provide the healing field—the depth of the Soul always knows the truth.

It can help and be a great blessing to have access to a Self-realized master who has attained this level of realization. But this too can be a challenge because just being in the presence of such souls (and the field they have established themselves in) acts as an accelerant and exposes those places within ourselves that need transformation. These "places" can be our own conscious or unconscious resistance to change, including thoughts, beliefs, behaviors, and attitudes that are not congruent with our Soul's highest expression. Staying on our path, digesting our experiences as best we can and to "keep on keeping on" is how we surmount the challenges.

If we do not have personal access to one who is Self-realized, then teachings in the form of writings produced by enlightened teachers and enlightenment teachings, past and present, can serve to give us inspiration, guidance, and direction—we can use our intuition and our discernment to find the information that is most appropriate and useful to us.

Most important of all is: no one can walk our path for us. It is up to each one, individually, to make the effort to dedicate him- or herself to evolving to a higher way of being…knowing too all the time that there is nothing to be achieved except the apprehension and unveiling of the Divinity that is already here in fullness.

In summary, this is what makes what we do different. As I wrote in Brain Sutra 5: people seeking to embody this presence must be on an "intense" path.

There is never a conflict with a person or condition, but rather a false concept mentally entertained "about" a person, thing or condition. Therefore make the correction within yourself, rather than attempting to change anyone or anything in the without.
    Joel Goldsmith, *The Art Of Spiritual Healing*

SILENT and amazed, even when a little boy,
I remember I heard the preacher every Sunday put God in his statements, As contending against some being or influence.
    Walt Whitman, "A Child's Amaze"

Brain Sutra 8

—⚊⚊—

The Big Picture: A Perspective on the Evolution of Ourselves and Humanity

According to Vedic literature, humanity goes through cycles of ascent and descent rather than a linear progression from less evolved to more evolved. This explains why there are so many mysteries from the past, remnants of ancient civilizations whose advanced knowledge and remains still cannot be satisfactorily explained by "modern" science. Stellar calculations with roots from perhaps 10,000 years ago show that our Milky Way galaxy revolves in an elliptical orbit around a grand central source. And just as the earth revolves around our sun and receives its life-giving radiations, so does our galaxy revolve around, and receive life-giving radiations from, the central source. The closer we are to the source, the more influential the emanations.

The orbit of our Milky Way galaxy takes 24,000 years around this source: 12,000 in an ascending cycle (moving toward the source) and 12,000 descending (moving away from the source). When our galaxy is in close proximity to the source in the elliptical path, the collective consciousness of humanity is receiving the highest degree of Divine light. This time period is known as a golden age

(Satya Yuga) in which peace, cooperation, and the spiritual qualities are predominant, affecting all levels of society, daily life, and existence. When we are the farthest from this point, the collective consciousness of humanity is considered to be in a dark age era with the inertia, chaos, discord, and primitive, instinctual attributes inherent to this period as the driving force. The peak of the last golden age was approximately 11,502 BC, the time of the great pyramids, Atlantis, and perhaps other forgotten but highly advanced great civilizations. The trough of the dark age was approximately 12,000 years later: 498 AD.

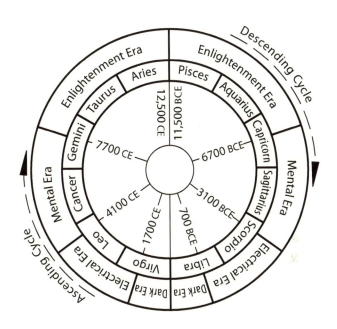

The ancient Vedic theory of the Yugas describes 24,000-year time cycles (Yugas), which are divided into four ascending and four descending stages of 12,000 years each. Sri Yukteswar related the Yugas to the movement of our solar system through the cosmos that is ellipsoid and repetitive in nature. Human consciousness is believed to be influenced by these stages: Kali Yuga (Dark Era), Dwapara Yuga (Electrical Era), Treta Yuga (Mental Era) and Satya Yuga (Enlightenment

Era or Golden Age). Consciousness is clouded in the Dark Era and then progressively clears to usher in the Enlightened Era when the majority of humanity is enlightened before the descending cycle begins anew. The current ascending Electrical Era started in 1700 C. E.

Along the ascending path, because of the gradual approach, the emanations from this grand source contribute to phases of greater and greater unfolding of knowledge moving from the dark age (Kali Yuga) to electrical/technological knowledge (Dwarpara Yuga)—to advances in mental powers and their application (Treta Yuga)—and finally to spiritual qualities at their peak during the truth age (Satya Yuga). In the descending cycle the collective consciousness of humanity again passes back through these phases in a deteriorating passage and finally enters the dark age before the galactic orbit again returns to the ascending path.

Currently our galaxy is ascending in Dwarpara Yuga (the electrical/technological age), moving away from the last dark era, Kali Yuga (702 BC to 1698 AD). The transition to Dwarpara Yuga occurred 1698 AD and history indeed corroborates a shift in the collective consciousness of humanity. There was a rapid influx of knowledge including inventions and discovery of the telescope, microscope, photography, X-ray, and other developments of the Renaissance period.

Although humanity as a whole is influenced by these dark periods, there are many enlightened individuals who come forth at all times and especially during these dark eras to connect with the Divine consciousness and remind humanity of its ultimate spiritual purpose. Christ, Krishna, Buddha and many other great lights all came forth during descending or dark eras to infuse humanity with the Divine will. The influence of space and time upon such individuals does not cloud their light. Indeed, if we so choose, as aspiring spiritual seekers our path is to overcome the inertia as well and awaken to our individual Divinity regardless of where we are in the cosmic cycle.

We have now moved three hundred years into this next phase, which brings forth knowledge that gives electrical and technological advancement. Also present now are allusions and glimpses of the next "mental" age, in which knowledge of the mind will bring us to profound advancements—as difficult for us to comprehend from our current view as space travel would have been for humanity five hundred years ago.

The next spiritual age where all of the planet and humanity will be imbued with Divine knowledge is 7698 AD. As we progress even at this early stage in 2015, more and more individuals are seeking spiritual answers to life's question. There is a struggle as we move forward, but the breaking free from the inertia of the dark era is visible all around us and is indeed inevitable.

As this electrical/technological age advances, we can observe that collectively, humanity is struggling to shift core values. If we measure humanity's progress by material gain, technological advancement and intellectual knowledge as reflected in how much we can gain, control, manipulate, dominate, and master the outer world, we miss the truth, the core principle, the purpose of what we are doing here. Technology is a great boon to mankind. But it can be used for negative, self-serving purposes.

We can wisely use technology to eradicate many of the world's challenges if our core principles are awakened and cultivated.

Therefore, what is most important is how much we each develop spiritually in our inner world regardless of what is happening around us. We can seek to replace competition, aggression, and division with the core principles of kindness, compassion, responsibility, and forward thinking. This is exclusively an inner process we individually cultivate. Our bodies contain primitive, instinctive traits programmed within our DNA from millions of years of evolution. These traits were for primitive survival and territorial protection, and they lead to aggression, unrest, tribalism, perverted religion, violence, and war. It is fruitless to try to change these traits in ourselves and others by shame, pressure, coercion, force, control, punishment, or other oppressive, manipulative, or aggressive means—these only produce the opposite force, resistance.

Focusing on our own personal spiritual growth is the key to cultivating a resonant response in the collective consciousness of humanity and will do more for the spiritual evolution of humanity than anything else. Therefore rather than looking at some group, faction, or culture "out there" and fault them, one can effect real growth and change the way Gandhi advised: "If we could change ourselves, the tendencies in the world would also change. As a man changes his own nature, so does the attitude of the world change towards him. ... We need not wait to see what others do."

How do we do this?

> Engage in spiritual disciplines.
> Practice superconscious meditation.
> In everything we do, cultivate the virtues.

We do not all need to be "world change activists" by pushing and struggling with humanity's inertia. This can of course be useful to draw attention to obvious sources that foster ignorance and stagnate the spiritual growth of humanity.

But by far, what will produce the most profound change in the collective consciousness of humanity is when we change ourselves—when we remove all that veils and clouds the radiance of our Soul—and when we awaken to our Divine purpose for being here.

Brain Sutra 9

Have You Had a Wake-up Call?

Sometimes life exposes and points things out to us in not-so-subtle ways, doesn't it? When there is resistance to the growth process and to our own personal evolution, we may have an unhealthy attachment to poor attitudes, self-limiting thoughts, petty beliefs, bad relationships, and self- destructive behaviors; in other words, an attachment to "life as we know it." Even if we know in our heart that life as we know it is not conducive to our highest good, we may hold on for lack of direction or lack of foreseeable options. Letting go and moving into the void of the unknown can be more threatening to our subconscious mind than staying in the unhealthy known. If this is the case, often life will send us some kind of message to shake us out of our slumber and force us to pay attention and make the necessary changes. If we refuse to pay attention and change, the message becomes more forceful and often has more severe consequences. We are all destined to wake up eventually, to learn our lessons and to release self-limiting thoughts…to do those important things we know deep down we should be doing for our own highest good and ultimate spiritual unfoldment. So why not make the move to wake up beforehand? Why not head off the wake-up calls by learning to be awake now?

At a certain turning point in our lives we may be compelled to ask the most important questions:

- Who am I?
- What is my purpose for being here?
- What is life?
- What is God, the Supreme Being, ultimate Reality?

These questions are a great blessing, often occurring in or after moments of a certain impetus: an event that shakes us and impels us to look past the transitory and superficial meanings and appearances to the deeper meaning of our existence. It can be a health crisis, a relationship gone awry, an accident, the passing of an acquaintance or loved one. There are also serious collective wake-up calls: world events that humanity is facing that include political, social, financial and environmental problems that we need to pay attention to because the consequences are mounting and are here now.

Many spiritual teachings have referred to this "shaking" as necessary to wake us up. Neuroscience research on advanced meditators indicates that when one enters an authentic spiritual path (one based on a systematic practice of spiritual discipline, meditation, cultivating the virtues, and surrendering the ego), over time the brain of the individual literally becomes more awake.

For the most part, the brain is an energy-conserving organ. There is a neural network called the default mode network (DMN) that functions as autopilot, keeping us from having to actively think about everything we do. Once something is learned, be it an attachment, aversion, or behavior, it is programmed in our brain's DMN and we do not have to think about it for future reference; it becomes automatic and requires no conscious thought. Much of the brain's energy and chemical resources (glucose, neurotransmitters, etc.) are doled out according to what our subconscious perception views as important events in our environment. The more of a shock, or out of the ordinary, the stimulus, the more awake our brain.

Great inspirational beauty and profound spiritual experiences trigger "awake" moments; however, so does trauma.

Some spiritual teachers point out that this brings us to an important point: In order for us to wake up (to begin the process of seeing and experiencing more than just a sleepwalking existence), it is necessary for us to recognize and realize that for the majority of the time we are indeed in a sleep condition. We need to make efforts to wake up on our own rather than be at the mercy of events in our lives that produce that shaking or the occasional inspirational moment.

Recent neuroscience research reveals a disturbing fact: for subjects studied, the average attention span is three seconds! Sounds discouraging to say the least! But do not be discouraged. Attention is a brain function and involves pathways in the brain; exercising these pathways can be compared to building stronger muscles—the more you exercise and train "attention" pathways, the stronger they will become. More and more areas of the brain will devote connections and neurons to this function if we know how to train it. This is crucial to understand if we are engaged in a spiritual growth process whose stages include practices that require us to learn to control and direct our attention.

The final goal of the stages of spiritual practice can be summed up in the following: We are, at the core of our being, pure awareness, or pure consciousness. This pure,

unconditioned state is behind our thoughts, behind our minds, behind our emotions, and is the silent witness. It is always here but because of the nature of our attention we do not experience this very subtle aspect of our being. Pure awareness is our very nature and is what is referred to as the "Self" or God, the Supreme Reality, manifesting as us. This is our deepest essence of being, and whether we are conscious of it or not, this is the Reality of our existence. The goal of spiritual practice is to remove all that clouds the superconscious experience of this.

This is why we have various spiritual paths that have been delineated over the ages. Sages, saints, and enlightened teachers have mapped out the process of awakening. Indeed, neuroscience is now corroborating this by documenting the physiological changes in the brain that occur as we go through the process of waking up.

> HAST never come to thee an hour,
> A sudden gleam divine, precipitating, bursting all these bubbles, fashions, wealth? These eager business aims—books, politics, art, amours,
> To utter nothingness?
> WALT WHITMAN, *LEAVES OF GRASS*

A spiritual teacher in the 1920s pointed out an obvious fact I mentioned earlier: Before one can awaken, one must first of all realize that most of the time, one is asleep. One must engage in a process that will help one to wake up. Why? There are many, many glorious things we miss in this sleeping state. If you have ever experienced a moment of true Reality, where Divinity is spontaneously recognized as a presence (and this presence in fact is *not* something separate from you, but your own presence) then you have had a glimpse of what lies beyond the autopilot state. The more powerful this Divinity is realized the more potent, overwhelming, and all-embracing the Divine love is…to the degree that this is experienced, one's life and world is touched and transformed beyond measure. This experience is here for all of us to live now—but to experience it for greater and greater periods requires brain changes. Again, that is what spiritual practices are for.

The phrase "be present" has become cliché. Unfortunately, the term has been overused and many people miss the profound implications of what it really means. Indeed, being awake requires that we learn to be present and all that this state implies—if we are simply not present to ourselves and to our environment then how can we consciously experience our own inner Divinity (our Self) which is always present? Because of the brain's DMN we are literally shutting off the pathways in the brain required for our attention and awareness to be present.

In Sanskrit the word used to define the state of consciousness when we are fully present and awake, when we are conscious of our Divinity and the Divinity as all that is, is *samadhi* (definition: "union" or "absorption"). When we begin to experience samadhi during superconscious meditation practice, our individual awareness is inwardly revealed and recognized as a unit of the total divine Presence. No separation—we are indeed one with God just as a drop of the ocean is one with the entire ocean.

The path, stages, or steps to samadhi are described as:

Attention > Concentration > Meditation > Contemplation > Samadhi

1. Awareness must be stabilized by strengthening attention: attention to being present.
2. Awareness can be focused, avoiding distractions and held to a point through concentration—gradually extending moments of being present.
3. Awareness is then directed deeper within and held steady in meditation, quieting the mind and going beyond mental fluctuations.
4. Awareness is directed toward an object, truth, idea, or knowledge in contemplation.
5. Awareness is turned back upon itself: "being aware of being aware" eventually leading to a progression through the levels of samadhi resulting in the highest states of conscious-

ness where subject and object merge. (The small "self" merges with the larger real "Self.")

I cannot stress enough that this process is a neurological process. Parts of the brain are refined so that the gradual training of awareness can progress through these stages.

The process of spiritual awakening is not just a metaphysical event and does not happen "out there somewhere." There are certainly transformations happening at subtler and subtler levels of our being; these are at the root of what we can measure in this physical/material level, and the subtle changes do reflect in our nervous system and physiology. It happens to, and in, our brains and this body temple.

The practices we have been given by the great spiritual adepts are to facilitate this process. At the Congress of World Religions in 1926, Paramahansa Yogananda said that the human nervous system and brain is the altar of God, and by refining it through spiritual practices one is naturally led within to the highest states of enlightenment, Self- and God-realization.

There is an important point regarding this whole process that is often missed or overlooked: to start, our awareness has to be trained. Our awareness is silent and witnessing, but gets pushed and pulled this way and that way by wherever our attention strays. Our awareness attaches itself to things, thoughts, and ideas (every three seconds!). Therefore, the first thing we must learn and train our brains to do is to practice being present: to train our awareness to stop attaching and identifying with thoughts, attitudes, and beliefs that are simply programmed into our brain's software. This is not easy. This requires training attention and a conscious directing of attention, beyond three seconds! There is tremendous inertia we must overcome to do this. Our brains want to do the opposite—our brains want to remain on autopilot.

I invite you to try something to verify this for yourself.

A Practical Exercise in Being Present

All work on oneself must be practical: it must give one a tangible, verifiable result. If it does not, then it is mere "theory" and "philosophizing"—what is referred to as "being in your head."

First release all notions and everything you have learned and heard about what it means to be present. It's important to start anew; clean the slate.

Being present begins as a very simple exercise in making efforts to be conscious of yourself in a given moment. The first thing we realize is just how difficult this is—I wake up in the morning and say to myself, "Today I will make efforts to be conscious, to be present." Then, that afternoon, for about five seconds, I remember this commitment I made and I wake up! But then it is the next day and I realize, "Oh my God, I completely forgot to be present since yesterday!" What happened?

The brain's DMN puts us back on autopilot, back to sleep. Try this yourself and you will be able to verify very quickly: it is very difficult and it requires a certain amount, and distinct quality, of energy to create moments of awake consciousness, of truly being present. And if we just depend on wake-up calls or on our own memory to remind us to be conscious and awake, we will often be discouraged.

Pick a day to try this:

Get a watch, or a timer, that has an alarm that you can set to sound every hour or two. For one full day, have this with you and when the alarm goes off, make an effort to be conscious, be present. Divide your attention between what is going on inside and what is going on outside. Conceptually try concentrating 66 percent of your awareness within and 33 percent without. Witness and observe the process. Do not judge, think, analyze, or do anything with your mind. Consciously use your attention to direct this process. The key to this is to be aware of your breath while you do this, for breath is always happening in the present. Observe the rhythm of your breath…breathe from your lower belly, and watch and be with your breath. Just be there. Observe and be aware of all your senses. Look and see the environment around you: hear it and feel it with your body. Be aware of being aware. If you can do this for three to four seconds, that is great! Try to gradually hold the state for five-plus seconds, but do not strain and do not get frustrated if you find it difficult. Your brain "muscle" has to build new pathways to do this, and that requires time.

After one day of this exercise, see how often you can remind yourself to do this, to be silently present-awake, without any external prompting. Over time you will experience more and more spontaneous moments of clarity and presence. This is the beginning of the awakening process and is the crucial first step to the gradual refinement of the brain and nervous system. Please try this. This exercise brings many interesting results—see for yourself.

Brain Sutra 10

Have You Had a Wake-up Call?

This Sutra is a continuation of the previous sutra—a discussion on the theme of Waking Up.

If you attempted the practice explained in Brain Sutra 9, "Have You Had a Wake-up Call?" you may have verified for yourself how difficult being present, and remembering to make efforts to be present, can be. Often we can go hours and days forgetting to give ourselves the nudge to wake up.

So the question arises: "Why is it so hard to be present?"

As I explained, primarily it is the brain's DMN that keeps us from thinking, keeps us on autopilot and keeps us from being present. If you tried the suggested exercise you may have discovered several things:

- It is hard to do and hard to remember to do.
- It is easier at certain times of the day when you have more energy.
- The state of "being present" has degrees: sometimes there is more clarity and sometimes less. *The degree of clarity is totally dependent on how much energy you have available.*

You can gauge how successful your efforts were by simply reviewing: Did you experience a moment that produced vivid memory—a conscious-present moment?

Those moments from our lives that we remember in complete vivid detail were moments when we were conscious-awake; it was in those moments that we were truly present. As mentioned in the last sutra, sometimes these moments are produced by shock or trauma, sometimes by seemingly normal influences, and other times by great beauty or spiritual inspiration. It is in these moments when we are truly Being; truly living. These moments create memory and we call them, "a conscious moment." We never forget the tangible Reality of feeling ourselves alive and existing in those instances.

Therefore, to cultivate the energy required for these moments we can:

1. Stop losing energy.
2. Learn to create energy.
3. Practice superconscious meditation.

1. Stop losing energy.

A primary loss of energy is through negative emotions. Every emotion you experience immediately affects every organ in your body. Anger, fear, insecurity, guilt, envy, anxiety, depression, jealousy, and worry are just some examples, but all negative emotions rapidly use up large portions of our energy reserves. It is this energy that can be channeled for higher states of consciousness. That is why we feel exhausted after a strong emotional stressor and why the root of many diseases can be traced to one or more significant life stressors. Our inability to handle negative emotion is also at the root of addiction. We self-medicate the uncomfortable feelings with food, alcohol, or other substances or behaviors.

Practice being present and awake when you are immersed in a negative state—this is the single most powerful thing we can do. Being awake can stop the leak and transform the reactive patterns that led to the negative state. Separate your awareness from the emotion and find the witness state—stand behind the emotion. Remind yourself that you are *having* a negative emotion, you *are* not the emotion.

Then to take it a step further, if it is appropriate, in order to literally chemically transform the negative energy/chemistry and the effects on your body, do the Inner Smile technique described at the end of this sutra.

The Inner Smile can help neutralize the cascade of destructive stress chemicals that occur. We can learn to literally transform negative emotions such as fear, doubt, and worry into strength and courage by applying this technique. Be sure not to suppress or deny negative emotions. That is like not having a release valve on a pressure cooker. The goal is to recognize that you *are* not the emotion, and transform or neutralize it.

Other ways we waste and use up energy include excessive talking, superficial forms of entertainment and stimulation, and addiction to excitement and sensations that give us a temporary feeling of being alive but leave us empty in the end.

Unconscious judgments of ourselves and others also deplete our energy reserves. Judgments never have a useful result. If we look upon others with compassion and we acknowledge the Divine essence of their being, we will find it impossible to judge, to be disappointed, or to get angry. The same applies to ourselves.

2. Learn to create energy.

All the impressions we take in during our day have specific qualities of energy and are registered consciously or unconsciously by our brains. Negative impressions give us negative energy, positive impressions give us positive energy. Once we understand this, we realize how very important it is to be intentional in regard to what we allow into our consciousness. Learn to avoid negative impressions especially when you are depleted, stressed, or tired.

Sources like the popular media, advertisements, news, TV, the internet, politics, and gossip can imprint unconscious messages if we are not careful. Did you know there is something called "neuro-marketing"? This is where marketing experts scan subjects' brains and figure out how to manipulate buying behavior by looking at the brain and nervous system. This information is then applied through marketing techniques as an attempt to coerce us to feel, believe (or sometimes fear) that we need that particular product. Politics use these methods as well.

Seek positive impressions. Be intentional about positive impressions too. These are impressions that give us energy and feed us with inspiration. The classic arts and the beauty of nature have much to offer. Great artistic works can provide us with a higher quality of impressions, whether they are paintings, statues, poetry, music, plays, books, or cathedrals, temples, monasteries, or other sacred places. All can have special qualities of energy that we can learn to appreciate and absorb. However, this does not necessarily happen automatically—it does not happen in sleep. The key to taking in the positive energy is to make efforts to be present at the moment one is observing the impression.

Over time we become more proficient, and the energy we need for greater awareness is readily available. We stop wasting energy, and the primitive-instinctual areas of the brain become less reactive to people and events that would have produced negative reactions in the past. Our lives take on a new vitality, new purpose and new meaning. Being calm, centered and nonreactive in all circumstances is perhaps the number one indication of spiritual growth and is the result of learning to be present-awake.

3. Practice superconscious meditation.

A recent study of the brains of advanced meditators showed that they are more awake, more present, and have much more refined awareness and perception. Each moment registers anew in the advanced meditator's brain—everything has great meaning and is filled with wonder and awe. Their brains indicated a predominance of a rhythm designated as gamma—these are very fast brain waves (40 hertz) and are founder in many times greater numbers than in the brain of. Gamma is a binding frequency in that it connects many areas of the brain and magnifies consciousness so that it is always new, always clear and always present, unbridled by the primitive-instinctual areas of the "older" brain regions. The test subjects had all practiced and used some form of the tools being shared here with you. The fundamental step to their transformation and state of consciousness is quite simple: this path begins and ends with "being present–being awake."

A seeker went to the Buddha and asked:

> SEEKER Sir, you seem to have achieved great spiritual heights. May I please enquire? Are you a god?
> BUDDHA No.

> SEEKER Are you the messiah?
> BUDDHA No.

> SEEKER Are you a king?
> BUDDHA No.

> SEEKER Are you enlightened?
> BUDDHA No.

> SEEKER Are you a perfected one?
> BUDDHA No.

SEEKER Well, then, what are you?
BUDDHA Awake.

The Inner Smile

The practice of the Inner Smile is not only reserved for a special place—the meditation room, place of worship, or other holy place. Nor should it be reserved for some special time when we are less distracted. Although our practices are important as support and respite for realigning ourselves, the life we live is the real field for the application of the Inner Smile. The practice can be brought into every situation and every relationship, consciously and with intention. First though, it can be useful to practice at the beginning of our superconscious meditation sessions in order to get a feel for the state. A guided audio version of the steps below is available on our website.

The Inner Smile requires a gentle shift in awareness: it is a state of alert-conscious-presence within and without. It is a state that is always available to us, silently underlying all that is occurring. To practice requires some effort because of the tendency for our attention to drift out of the present moment and engage in the workings of the mind and events happening around us. Identification with the mind and its contents keeps us from experiencing the consciousness that illumines the mind. By making efforts to remind ourselves to smile internally: to be simultaneously aware of the life force that is expressing through us and manifesting as everything around us, although an intellectual exercise at first, eventually becomes a living state of smiling awareness. The simplest things in life then reflect great beauty and grace...we are no longer bound by the conditionings of the mind, i.e. the labels, judgments or preconceived notions, but rather, we see the world in a new light as it is, without our projections.

1. Begin by gathering "smiling energy" behind your eyes.

2. Let this energy permeate your brain, then move it down into your body through your nervous system.
3. Smile to all your internal organs, bones and cells of your body—then smile to the whole universe and all beings everywhere.

Brain Sutra 11 – Part 1

—∞—

Navigating Through the Layers of the Mind

Every person, at the center of their being, is pure unconditioned awareness; an individualized unit of Divine consciousness. So why do we not consciously experience this all the time?

Visualize your Divine essence as a sphere; around it are layers and layers representing the subconscious mind, with a final, outside layer representing the conscious mind. This illustrates our expression from the inside out. The outer layers are like clouds and are where the various conditionings reside that obscure the purity of our awareness as it flows out to the external world—but at the source it remains ever the same.

Depending on our individual subconscious conditionings, our thoughts, beliefs and behaviors are modified accordingly. The purity of our Soul is always here, the subtlest of the subtle, always conscious, always clear—it is always in the background, witnessing all our states of consciousness (even in the deepest sleep stages). We do not achieve, deserve, or earn our Divinity. The "I am" of us is already one with omnipresent Divinity…always has been, always will be. Our path, if we are so inspired, is to redirect the outward flow of our awareness and to inquire within, "Who am I?" This inner questioning will ultimately reveal the same truth for us all. Every Soul, in this life or in another, is destined to discover this. Studying books, teachings, or following teachers cannot give us this awareness—they can only point the way. Only our diligent inner seeking, learning to quiet and calm the mind and clear away the clouded layers of the subconscious, can lead us to the inner unveiling and realization of our true being.

It can be useful to understand the layers of the subconscious that cloud awareness and how we can manage and navigate through them. Contemporary psychology has relatively little to offer us in regard to reaching our highest potential as spiritual beings. Psychotherapy can help us manage our "human" problems: our relationship issues, neurosis, and the day-to-day problems and challenges, but does little to give us the tools that will provide us with the answers to life's greatest mysteries. We can look to authentic enlightenment teachings for these answers. This information comes from individuals who have gained access to their higher mind, the superconscious mind. Most contemporary psychological theories do acknowledge unconscious and subconscious levels of mind but do not recognize the highest potential of the superconscious mind. In order to comprehend this higher Reality we must first accept it as a possibility and then engage in spiritual practices that have been passed down over millennia so that we may experience this. These practices have been tested and proven and have allowed individuals to reach the highest states of Self- and God-realization. We, through these practices, can begin to glean the potential of spiritual unfoldment—and move beyond just wanting to become more psychologically "normal" and have stress-free lives. There is nothing wrong with "normal" or seeking a stress-free life. In fact, becoming more psychologically sound and growing into emotional maturity is part of, and the result of, our spiritual growth. We become more responsible, learn to make a real contribution to our world and become more functional in all areas of our daily lives. As we follow the spiritual teachings and disciplines, cultivate the virtues, and apply them in our lives, the healing, balancing and harmonizing of our lives and personalities will inevitably occur along the way.

The Levels of the Mind

The mind has conscious, subconscious, and superconscious levels.

The Conscious Mind

What we believe to be our conscious mind is somewhat of an illusion.

Interacting and engaging in life and the world around us, we believe our motivation, judgments, thoughts, intellect, and decisions are being determined from our conscious, rational mind. But in truth our conscious mind is being driven by our subconscious conditionings. The conditionings include ideas, concepts, and beliefs: everything we assume to be true and have learned about ourselves and the world around us. Learning occurs when information first passes through our conscious mind and, if accepted, gets stored in our subconscious and programs our brain—the brain's autopilot, default mode network (DMN), is imprinted with the information. We then believe and behave accordingly, perhaps never really examining the basis of the information and determining if the information we stored away is true. The question is: What is the source of the concepts and beliefs our brain's software has accepted as truth? If we examine the sources we may find that, yes, there are some obvious facts and things that are true. But in regard to many concepts and beliefs, much of what we hold to be true is just someone else's opinion—and this could include information that came from less-than-enlightened minds. The only information we want to accept into our minds, and hence into our subconscious, is that which is accurate and enlightened. Enlightened information that emerges from the superconscious as a result of spiritual practice is higher knowledge. The source of this higher knowledge is Self-revealed and is unveiled as we learn to access the superconscious level of our inner being.

The Subconscious Mind

The subconscious is the storehouse of the impressions we take in. Everything we have experienced is a memory recorded electrochemically in our brain and body.

The beliefs that make up the content of the subconscious are like a magnet and attract circumstances that confirm them and reflect back to us as our outer lives. In a sense the subconscious projects out and attracts what we call the good and bad things in our lives. In this way our experiences are self-created. If the subconscious impressions are negative we will have corresponding experiences until we eradicate the wrong or harmful subconscious belief. Success too is a manifestation of subconscious conditioning. The problem though, is most of the time we are unconscious of this principle. Our minds tell us, "Things happen," but in truth things can only happen according to our subconscious beliefs. Learning to recognize the subconscious impressions is the key to releasing the unfavorable conditionings and a first step to gaining more conscious access to the superconscious level.

A popular theme among the new age community is around the notion of reprogramming the subconscious. If our goal is to awaken to the Reality of our being and to consciously experience our Divinity, then reprogramming is not a good idea. That just creates more mental impressions and more mind stuff that has to eventually be cleared away. The subconscious cannot be programmed to experience the Divine essence—the Divine essence is behind the subconscious and is what we refer to as the superconscious. Unconditioned pure awareness is our real identity. Anything else just obscures this. So clearing away the subconscious impressions that are not useful is the proper approach; but first we have to learn how to recognize the impressions and the manifestation of them in our lives, to make our subconscious transparent.

Learn to observe your subconscious. Make it transparent. Take just a minute the next time you are in a public place, driving, shopping, or eating, and try to observe your mental chatter... notice the background internal conversation going on in your mind. You may notice a running commentary on people and things, sometimes an internal dialogue, occasional judgments and pre-judgments toward others. It can be very revealing and give a notion of how much is actually going on in the subconscious that is almost totally outside of conscious awareness. Notice if there is anything habitual that you do or think, a judgment about a certain type of person or a persistent attitude that you may not have noticed before. If you can do this you are witnessing the play of your subconscious mind as it projects its contents onto the outside world. When we are not consciously being present our subconscious colors all our perceptions according to its content and beliefs.

If we continue to observe ourselves, over the course of time, many of us will begin to identify the contradictions between our conscious and subconscious mind. Our conscious mind tells us we believe and behave in certain ways, but if we can be present and observe we will see that oftentimes this is not the Reality. We "know" better than we "do." This requires keen observation and being very honest with ourselves. We have internal mechanisms that keep us from the discomfort of seeing that what we find most annoying and disturbing in others is usually a prominent feature in ourselves—just unrecognized. Our judgments of others, complaints of unhappiness with the world and other people's weakness or behaviors is usually because we see this reflected in ourselves. When we discover these inconsistencies we do not want to start judging ourselves but rather practice compassion. If we can have compassion for ourselves the same principle applies and we will see this compassion extended and reflected to the world and people around us too—judgments will cease. But first we have to practice being conscious and alert to our own inconsistencies—this is what is meant by making the subconscious transparent.

Often simply reading the type of information contained in this sutra will pull on the subconscious and information and in-sight will be brought into your conscious mind awareness. Because of this it is useful to read this sutra several times over the course of several days, and you will experience more and more insight. Dreams also provide a look, symbolically, into the contents of the subconscious. If you become aware of subconscious conditioning, beliefs, attitudes, thoughts or behaviors that are not conducive to your highest good, the practical exercise outlined in the next sutra, Clearing the Subconscious, will help.

The Superconscious Mind

The inner source in each one of us that gives us our hunches, our intuitions, our inner guidance, higher knowledge and higher revelation is the superconscious mind.

Great inventions, discoveries, and breakthroughs are not just the result of individual genius or brilliance but rather of individuals gaining access to this level of "brilliance," of superconscious knowledge. We do not each have a personal superconscious mind—the superconscious mind is one. It is universal, sometimes called the oversoul, the mind of God, and we are a portion of the one mind at the level of superconsciousness. All knowledge resides here...not in books, not outside ourselves but within each one of us. When we read a spiritual truth over and over and then suddenly we understand it for the first time, the understanding is a recognition of what we already know within—the book just helped remind you—your teacher is your own realization. This is a level of pure potentiality, stillness and infinite knowledge. When we learn to go within, silence the mind and touch the superconscious level, we tap into a "peace that passeth understanding" and begin to experience an outpouring of infinite Divine knowledge and inspiration. The etymology of the word *inspiration* is from *inspire*: to inhale or breathe in. Great spiritual adepts say that the ancient scriptures were "realized" within and recorded. The way to the superconscious requires us to clear away the subconscious conditionings that cloud our inner vision. This is why superconscious meditation is the primary tool recommended in virtually all enlightenment traditions. We go within and within and within... passing through the layers of the subconscious until we reach the point of profound stillness—we become aware of being aware.

In the next sutra, Navigating Through the Layers of the Mind (Part 2): Clearing the Subconscious, this theme will be continued. But first reread this sutra a few times at your convenience and practice the exercise described above.

Brain Sutra 11 – Part 2

Clearing the Subconscious

The mind is like an iceberg. As in an iceberg, 90 percent of the mind submerged and is what we call the subconscious, with 10 percent being the "surface" conscious mind. The 90 percent is most influential and is where our life scripts are stored. These are electrochemical impressions in the brain created by events that define our self-identity, our likes and dislikes, and what motivate what we consider to be our "conscious" behavior. In yoga science these subconscious conditionings are called *samskaras*: the mental impressions that cloud our awareness of our true nature as divine Being.

To clear the subconscious we must acknowledge the truth and affirm the truth. Follow these steps.

Acknowledge the Truth

1. First and foremost always acknowledge, remember, and understand that you are one with divine being: flawless, perfect and pure at your core.
2. Do an inventory. Resolve memories of past negative experience. Face and neutralize uncomfortable and difficult mem-

ories by defusing the emotional reaction to the memory. You will know when you are done when the physical reaction to the memory, such as anxiety, remorse, insomnia, addictive cravings, depression, rapid heartbeat, cold sweats, ceases. When you no longer have a physical or emotional reaction to the memory then the memory has been neutralized.

If you suspect there are things you cannot recognize in yourself, or that you do not remember from the past, then over a few days reread this sutra. Talk less, observe yourself more, and your subconscious will begin to release and reveal to you memories, repetitive patterns, wrong beliefs and unproductive behaviors that come from past incidents and subconscious conditioning.

3. Throw out the trash: Use the ancient Vedic ritual known as **Vasana Daha Tantra**.[1]

When memories emerge from your subconscious of past hurts, hurts toward others, mistakes made, regrets, trauma, guilt, fear, anxiety, worry, self-doubt, or unworthiness, write them down in as much detail as possible. If there are ways these memories are influencing your life now and there are certain behaviors in your life that you know are not your best, write them down too. Do not type but write in cursive—this is important as this encourages access to deeper brain regions. Be specific and give as much detail as you can. Be honest with yourself. If there is a lesson to be learned, face it, learn it, make a commitment to end any unacceptable behaviors and then allow yourself to let it go and move on. Then burn the paper. This is an ancient method used to clear the subconscious using the symbolism of burning the accumulated negative "mind-stuff" in

---

[1] *Vasana* means "subliminal/subconscious traits that are manifesting now." *Daha* means "to blaze." *Tantra* means "technique, instrument, or method of applying higher knowledge to tie/weave together."

written form. Your subconscious will recognize the symbolism here—it may require several attempts to clear the conditioning but eventually you will experience the desired changes. Be diligent and write out those things you want to release when you are aware of them. Don't give up! Be aware too that this is not an auspicious "sacred fire" ritual. The instructions are to use an appropriate container to burn the paper, such as a trash can!

Why do we resist change? We may inadvertently hold on to much of our subconscious conditionings for a number of reasons. It may be that they are the "known" and define and support our identity. Most of our behaviors are simply re-action: mechanical responses to life that are laid down in our brain's software—determined by our past. Many of the conditionings are not in line with our highest good: they were perhaps imposed upon us by people who taught us or cared for us and/or whom we respected. There is often a feeling of safety and protection at the root of many of our conditionings, and releasing them (at first) can make us feel less safe.

Instinctive areas of the brain are programmed for survival and can have enormous resistance to surrendering to an unknown future. We may have received negative messages in our early childhood which can create deep impressions and be the most challenging to release because they have become so much a part of our identity.

Addictions, too, have subconscious roots and are tied to neurochemical forces that drive the addiction. Addiction to a behavior is not really due to the behavior itself but rather to the rush of brain chemicals associated with the behavior—the neurotransmitter dopamine is the primary pleasure/motivator in most addictions—in this sense our subconscious learns to self-medicate by using a substance or a behavior as a source of relief from negative or uncomfortable feelings.

Post-traumatic stress disorder (PTSD) is also a "conditioning of the subconscious": the result of trauma triggering primitive areas of the brain that afterward cannot turn off the surveillance, remaining hypervigilant, ever on the alert to any threat of danger. The severity of conditioning that occurs with PTSD requires a much more comprehensive approach. Currently there are very successful therapeutic programs using meditation, neurofeedback, yoga, and similar supportive tools to gently turn off the subconscious conditioning.

If you cannot understand why you have trouble releasing something, such as a behavior, attitude, or relationship, ask yourself, "What does holding onto this particular conditioning do for me?"

Many of us have resistance to growth and to emotional maturity. Resistance to emotional maturity is perhaps the number one obstacle to our spiritual growth. There are many people walking around in bodies that are many years older than their emotional age, sometimes decades. We can get emotionally stuck at developmental levels and have the emotional maturity corresponding to those ages. We may have experienced a trauma, parents' divorce, separation, or other unsettling circumstance that slowed or shut down our emotional growth. We can break the chains to the past by practicing being present, conscious, and awake here and now.

In time, through honest self-inquiry, the answer to the question, "Why do I resist change and what is holding me back?" will reveal itself, enabling you to face it and move on.

Many times the realization is surprisingly simple: moving on (or not) is basically a choice.

Be clear though, that this is not a process of psychoanalysis; psychoanalysis can be an endless loop. Rather, this is a process intended to allow your consciousness to rise above, or move beyond, this level of the mind in order to access the superconscious level. This gives us a higher view and a "pure" understanding.

By making the subconscious transparent, by recognizing and exposing its contents and their manifestation both good and bad in our lives, we can then begin to consciously experience the unveiling of the superconscious. Ever increasing glimmers of light, of a higher way of knowing and being, will shine forth from the superconscious. This ultimately brings about liberation and freedom from all that restricts and all that clouds the radiance of the Soul.

Affirm the Truth

Create an affirmation that is the truth, the Reality at the Soul level. Affirmation is not meant to reprogram the subconscious but rather to give the subconscious accurate and enlightened information. Affirmations should be short, positive, and motivating. Think of your affirmation as an antidote to any negative conditionings you identify and word it accordingly.

Three crucial ingredients to successful affirmation:

1. Focus, think, and give full attention to the affirmation as you repeat it. Do not let the mind wander.
2. Visualize a mental picture with as many sensory components as possible to illustrate your affirmation. What colors are present? What sensations? What sounds? What odors? What are the physical feelings?
3. Feel it! Bring all the positive emotion, gratitude, joy, and appreciation into your realization and actualization of your affirmation.

Practice your affirmation for a few minutes after waking, again before lunch, before bed, and if you awaken in the night. When you meditate, bring the affirmation in at the end of your meditation session. Do this for a while and then if inspired try a new affirmation. A good goal is to repeat your affirmation for at least fifty repetitions per day.

Favorite affirmations:
- Everything in my mind, everything in my consciousness, everything in my world is in Divine order.

- I am healthy, vital, and radiantly alive.
- I am calm, confident, and serene.
- The radiant purity of my essence of Being continuously illumines my mind and consciousness.
- I am all right, right now.

You can either walk through a city full of fog or climb above it.
SUBRAMUNIYASWAMI (1927–2001)

Brain Sutra 12

Truth

You never have and never will be separate from Supreme Being; indeed, it is not possible. This oneness is not earned, achieved, or deserved, nor is it available only to spiritual or religious people. Whether we are conscious of this or not, it is the truth. Everyone and everything is divine Being. This is what existence is—the manifestation of Divine consciousness. The nature of Divine consciousness is existence-consciousness-bliss. Consciousness is self-aware of existence and this is experienced as bliss. Simple, profound, present, and silent—the "I am." Everywhere present, the only power, and all-knowing (omnipresent, omnipotent, omniscient). Therefore, there is nothing other than that—it is the essence of individual consciousness. There is not a universe of matter *and* a Supreme Being—the universe *is* the Supreme Being. All feelings of separation, fear, doubt, anxiety, worry, and belief in "evil" are disqualified when the absolute truth is unveiled. Spiritual paths simply help the individual to see what is already here. We are already fully Divine. The invisible essence that is at the core of your reading this is the same invisible essence that is at the core of my writing this. Our ego and personalities may tell us otherwise… but nevertheless, the truth is what it is, and ultimately every Soul will realize this.

Our task is to correct our minds' incorrect translation of ourselves and the world around us in order to allow the Divine Reality to be comprehended. When this happens, it is as if awakening from a dream. We cannot know the supreme with our mind as if it were a concept. A concept is objective to us—external to us. We can only experience it or be it in Reality.

The question naturally arises, if there is the ultimate ever-present Divinity within everyone and everything, then why is there the suffering we see in the world and the heinous acts committed human-against-human, against other living things and even against the planet itself? What divine Being would allow this?

First we have to correct any false definitions of what divine Being is. Many of us were taught that God is a human-like (anthropomorphic) being sitting up in heaven somewhere at a distance, making judgments and doling out punishment or grace and blessings depending on what we deserve. God cannot be defined as external to us, and therefore cannot be known with the mind. The mind and its contents must be quieted in order to get behind it: to experience the divine Source. Since this truth is somewhat incomprehensible to the mind we have invented various definitions throughout history. Some of us have rejected a belief in divine Being altogether which, when Divinity is realized, is amusing because, "What is rejecting what?" There are many, many human notions, names, attributes, and concepts projected by us on this very simple, in essence, presence we call God, Supreme Being. It is what it is regardless of the names we give it. Questioning or being angry at God for allowing suffering is like being angry at the sun for shining equally on the weeds in our garden and letting them grow too!

The life force of you and me and everything: literally the vitality you feel coursing through your nervous system animating you, that enables you to live, to breathe, and to know you are you, this consciousness you see behind everyone's eyes, animals included, and if you are sensitive, in all things, is the divine Being manifesting. Impartial, impersonal, equally present in all but not fully conscious in all—at least not in terms of our definition of "conscious." From the mineral kingdom, to primitive organisms, to the vegetable kingdom, to the animal kingdom, to human (and beyond) are all different levels of the manifestation of one supreme Divine intelligence.

However, the human nervous system, and its subtle components, is unique on this planet in that it is the medium that allows us to comprehend the Divine Reality within when we have the correct information and guidance.

God plays all the roles. What appears as suffering, struggle, strife, and evil is just due to degrees of ignorance: relative degrees of the clouding of Divinity—sometimes called "unknowing." As our "knowing the truth" becomes more and more established, steady, and unshaken, we are transformed by the unfolding of the Reality that is always here. Intellectual understanding becomes experiential, and our perception of ourselves and the world is transformed.

The Truth

I salute the supreme teacher, the Truth, whose nature is bliss, who is the giver of the highest happiness, who is pure wisdom, who is beyond all qualities and infinite like the sky, who is beyond words, who is one and eternal, pure and still, who is beyond all change and phenomena and who is the silent witness to all our thoughts and emotions—I salute the Truth, the supreme teacher.

Ancient Vedic Hymn

Brain Sutra 13

—∞—

The Origin and the Science of Superconscious Meditation

Science without religion is lame, religion without science is blind.

ALBERT EINSTEIN

Science is defined as, "a systematically organized body of knowledge on a particular subject."[2]

Meditation is perhaps the oldest and greatest science. The teachings have existed for many thousands of years organized as a systematic approach to harmonizing the body, mind, and emotions with the goal being eventual transcendence of the mind and the emergence of higher states of consciousness (known as superconsciousness). Meditation is not exclusive to any one religion or path but rather is a spiritual practice and as such, is meant to facilitate one's awareness of oneself as spiritual Being. Contemporary scientific investigation is now documenting the far-reaching physical, personal, and collective benefits of regular meditation practice.

---

[2] As defined by the Oxford Dictionaries

Yoga science, the source of meditation teaching, is gaining more and more recognition as a body of profound knowledge. Its roots are in the ancient Vedas—the oldest of world scripture. Some estimate the Vedas at 6,000 to 8,000 years old and others date them as far back as 10,000 years. The Vedas contain a vast array of information that was only written down, translated, and understood on a larger scale this past century. Since antiquity this enormous storehouse of information was passed on purely as an oral tradition from teacher to student. The Vedas contain symbolism and hidden meaning veiling profound truths. They were created during the declining portion of last golden age (Satya Yuga) as a vehicle to transmit higher knowledge to subsequent civilizations so it would not be lost. The Rishis (seers) who recorded the Vedas knew of the impending dark age but also knew that there would be a cyclical return to an enlightened age in the distant future and there would be people of higher mind who would intuitively grasp the keys to unlock the hidden meaning. As the mystery of the Vedas are understood and revealed there is an entire range of spiritually based science and knowledge covering everything from health to government being resurrected and made available.

When most westerners hear the term *yoga* they think of hatha yoga, commonly known as the system of poses or postures (asanas). This particular portion of yoga science is meant as a preliminary step to harmonize the energies of the physical body so the eventual quieting of the mind and subsequent meditation practices can ensue. However, hatha yoga, according to scholars, is a fairly recent development evolving much later than the original Vedic texts—perhaps just a few hundred years old. As time goes on, those who are practicing hatha yoga will glean the deeper philosophy of yoga science. The word yoga means to "yoke or join together" referring to the merging of the individual self with Divine consciousness—that is the goal of yoga practice. A recent documentary film entitled, *Awake!*, concerning the life of the great teacher Paramahansa Yogananda, had an apropos statement in it referring to the potential body obsession many "yoga" advocates fall into, "Yoga is not about flat abs (and fashionable outfits)!" Indeed as the depth of yoga science becomes more and more understood, the core and profundity of the teachings will ultimately be recognized. Yoga has different aspects with different emphases, including raja yoga, bhakti yoga, jnana yoga, karma yoga, and many others, but they all lead to the same ultimate truth.

In the previous sutras, the importance of the state referred to as superconsciousness and the practice of superconscious meditation is emphasized. Discovering how to recognize and access superconsciousness is facilitated through the regular practice of superconscious meditation. Yoga science teaching provides the clearest and most effective instruction for moving through the layers of the mind as we progress in our meditation practice.

As a daily practice for de-stressing and spiritual anchoring this can be the single most important thing you can do for yourself. There are currently hundreds of studies detailing the vast benefits of regular meditation practice—immune boosting, better sleep, eliminating addictions, reduced depression and anxiety, more compassion, slowing down the aging process, effects on overall well-being to name just a few. There is even research reporting that a collective field is created when a number of people meditate together and has measurable effects in reduced crime rates in the vicinity. People close to you benefit from your increasing centeredness and life naturally flows more smoothly and effortlessly as superconscious levels are experienced. (If you are not clear about superconsciousness go back and reread Sutra 11.)

Make an appointment with yourself for your practice and find time every day to devote to this most essential routine. The best time for meditation is usually before sunrise if your schedule permits. If you need to, go to bed a little earlier and arise earlier so that you can allow twenty to forty-five minutes before your day starts for your practice. Eat a light dinner at least three hours before bed the night before and avoid alcohol or caffeine so that your sleep is deep and your mind is as clear as possible for your early morning meditation session—this can make an enormous difference if you experience "heaviness" upon awakening. If you are familiar with

Ayurveda then follow the Sattvic dietary recommendations. A Sattvic[3] diet is conducive to a physiology that supports a balanced body chemistry and a clear mind in order to enhance meditation practice.

Start slow. If you are new to meditation, five to ten minutes to begin with is fine. Surrendered prayer or reading devotional or inspirational literature can be useful too during this time, especially when the mind is resistant to quieting. Just make the time and sit no matter what.

Don't get frustrated—eventually meditation becomes something you are drawn to, not as an escape, but as a profound opportunity to experience your essence of being—superconsciousness. Using a guided meditation audio in the beginning is all right, but eventually your goal is to be self-directed. Meditation music as well as any external distractions should also be avoided when you internalize attention. There are even apps now to help beginning meditators. As preliminary supportive tools these are fine if they help prepare, quiet, and calm the mind. However, the inner silence is where our attention is ultimately directed.

How to Practice Superconscious Meditation

3 "Sattvic foods are soothing, nourishing, and promote and maintain a quiet, steady mind as well as help to sharpen your intellect and give you a greater sense of empathy. Sattvic foods are vegetarian and do not include foods derived from animals that have been harmed in any way. It is important that foods are grown naturally and do not contain preservatives, artificial flavors, or additives." — YogaBasics.com

1. Regulate your breath. Turn your attention to the inhalation and exhalation. Breathe from your belly (diaphragmatic breathing) making the length of your inhalation and exhalation approximately equal. Do not force or strain. Simple, slow, rhythmic breathing is the objective. Maintain this breath awareness throughout your meditation session.
2. Feel grounded to the earth. It is important when we meditate that we make conscious contact with the earth. We are temporary residents of these physical bodies and of this earth. Our bodies are made of the substance of the earth and stars and are akin to transmission towers on this planet. We are as much a part of nature as every other living thing on this planet and just as involved in all its cycles. Our bodies are conduits through which a vast cosmic cycle of energy flows from many dimensions of space and time, the stars, our galaxy, our sun, our planets, our moon, and our earth. Our eyes can only perceive one tenth of a billion of the total information that rides on this electromagnetic spectrum of energy.

Try this: If you have been sitting cross-legged for meditation, try putting your feet flat on the floor while sitting in a chair and instead of having the earth energy go right up into your spine, allow it to flow through the soles of your feet. This way the earth energy is refined as it travels through various meridians along the legs before it enters the spinal pathway. This can help you feel more stable, present, grounded and less "spacey." Being dreamy, spacey or ungrounded is to be avoided. True meditation is a conscious-alert-aware state, keenly perceptive and highly functional.

1. Invoke or acknowledge your relationship as one with the infinite. Start your meditation sessions with some kind of acknowledgment, invocation, and awareness of the ever-

presence of the Infinite, Supreme Being. Also acknowledge your teacher(s) if you have any, at the beginning of the meditation. If you pray, pray with surrendered devotion not as a petition but rather for awareness of your real nature as pure being.

2. Direct attention to the spiritual eye; stay focused and still. The spiritual eye, also known as the third eye, in its location at the center of the forehead corresponds to the prefrontal lobes of the brain. This is a very important area of the brain as it is the seat of higher- order thinking, concentration, and focus: the executive functions of the brain. Therefore try to keep your attention there when you meditate. When the eyes are focused on one point and held steady, the steady gaze will contribute to steady concentration. If you are having trouble concentrating when you are meditating, pay attention to where your eyes are focusing. When your gaze drops below the horizon, you tend toward more distracted, daydreaming, and potentially subconscious states. If you are falling asleep when you meditate keep your gaze up, as if you are looking up and out through that point at the center of your forehead with eyelids closed. If you see internal visions, faces, geometric patterns, flowing colors or glowing light, no matter what the phenomena, keep directing your awareness "through or beyond" to the source. If your body is restless, just keep redirecting it to be still. Every time you move, your brain is stimulated to a degree. Therefore, being physically still is important, but don't repress your natural need to make occasional shifts for comfort.

4. Use a mantra. Introduce a mantra "mentally listened to" with inhalation and exhalation. The inhalation and exhalation should be approximately the same length. There should be no pauses between inhalation and the exhalation. Do not mentally repeat, or repeat out loud, but rather "listen" to it

in your mind. The purpose of the mantra is, with focused repetition, to eventually allow the thoughts to settle so that you can experience pure awareness beyond thought. A widely used Sanskrit mantra is *hong-sau*. For example, mentally listen to "hong" as you inhale, "sau" as you exhale.

5. When the mind quiets, disregard the mantra. Rest in the calm alert (Superconscious) state for as long as you can. It is in that state that the healing occurs and that the transformation process is accelerated. Superconsciousness is tangible. It may take some time, but when you reach it, you will know when you experience it. It is a profound quiet thoughtless state—pure awareness. It is already present within you but clouded by mental impressions and subconscious conditioning. It is also referred to as the fourth state of consciousness, from which you witness the other three states.

6. Before concluding, expand your awareness to embrace infinite space and radiate compassionate goodwill to all beings everywhere.

7. End your meditation session with deep gratitude and appreciation.

Brain Sutra 14

—∞—

Get into the Gap

Ramification: an accidental consequence that complicates things.

When our thoughts are subconsciously driven there tend to be many unintended ramifications. One thought leads to the next, makes a diversion; another subject or memory is added and before we realize it; our thoughts seem out of control or at least take an unintended (or apparently aimless) path. Endless-loop thinking, too, is the result of thoughts going in circles by this ramification process: we search for a solution to an issue, but our search may just end up back where we started.

How does this happen? Where or what is it in the brain that is driving this thought process? The answer lies within the intricate network of communication between sending and receiving cells.

Cells do not directly connect one with another. Instead there are junctions between them called synapses which are basically gaps. This applies to all the cells in the body including brain, organs, and tissues. A message is only delivered when the sending cell has enough electrochemical force behind it—otherwise the message simply is not carried on to the receiving cells. Once the message successfully crosses the gap, the receiving cell transfers it on through electrochemical transmissions to other cells. The key lies in this gap and in the messengers whose job it is to shuttle the information back and forth. When the message makes it across the gap, this is referred to as "activation" and when they do not this is called "inhibition." The chemical messengers in the gap are called neurotransmitters because their job is to transmit the nerve messages. The late Candace Pert called neurotransmitters "the molecules of emotion." There are many neurotransmitters, but the most important appear to be serotonin, dopamine, and GABA. Serotonin is associated with well-being, appetite, sleep, and many other functions—90 percent of serotonin is in the GI tract. Dopamine is the "pleasure and reward" neurotransmitter; it drives us toward people, events, or things in our environment that are attractive and modifies our behavior accordingly through a pleasurable feeling (chemistry) of "reward." Addiction to behaviors such as overeating, gambling, or sex is really addiction to our own body's dopamine stimulation and not really to the behaviors themselves. GABA (gamma-aminobutyric acid) acts as an inhibitor in the brain and nervous system, the body's own tranquilizer. Medications in the benzodiazepine class are GABA mimickers and if used over the long term can have deleterious side effects.

The gap between cells is analogous to the gap between thoughts. Pause for a moment with that awareness. (You are experiencing the gap when you pause.)

As stated above, our thoughts, when subconsciously driven, tend to be self-propelling, one on top of the other. The consequence is a repetition and a deepening of perception and ways of thinking (like grooves in a record). This repetition reinforces learned ways of thinking and learned behaviors, worldviews, attitudes, and beliefs that lie deep within the subconscious. This is why change is so difficult for many people. This is the imprinting in our cell networks referred to in previous sutras as the DMN (default mode network), the brain and body's autopilot.

Behavior modification and other psychological approaches to change often help some, but for others the challenge of changing deeply held belief systems can be a daunting project. Indeed, many of us struggle our entire lifetime with patterns we know are not for our highest good. There is also the effect of collective beliefs, beliefs held by religion, culture, science, medicine, and society that influence us daily. This is actually quite dangerous, because with the presence of almost instantaneous media our opinions and beliefs about life, about what gives us happiness, and the political, environmental, social, and economic views of the world around us are constantly being influenced and manipulated by minds whose motives may not always be in our best interest (or the best interest of our planet). All this influences the gap—whether we know it or not—and must be made conscious so that we do not blindly accept that which is unacceptable, false, harmful, or erroneous.

For as he thinketh in his heart, so is he.

PROVERBS 23:7

Why is it that some people heal miraculously? How do we explain the incredible changes we know the human body is capable of? Is it simply unexplainable? The answer is in the profound realization of the Reality that "we are what we think." And this takes us back to the gap.

There is supporting evidence that the DNA within our cells is informed by the neurotransmitters crossing the gap. The DNA carries the blueprint for the architecture of our body and for each individual cell. That means the messages, good or not-so-good, in terms of stress or well-being (literally what is happening in the gaps) determine the information that our cells receive. As an example, if we are experiencing stress and our neurotransmitters relay this message, the cells will respond and be affected accordingly. If we are experiencing well-being, the cells will receive those chemical messages.

This affects the health of our cells, organs, tissues, our immune function, including autoimmune, and to a degree, even the gene expression of certain genetic diseases. So how do we take a conscious role?

Again: The gap between our cells is analogous to the gap between our thoughts. Pause for a moment with that awareness. (You are experiencing the gap when you pause.)

When we experience the quiet-neutral-silent conscious state of presence we are in pure potentiality—the gap is in pause mode between thoughts. In this pause we are the essence of our being—the absolute unified field of consciousness—the Divinity within—superconscious. From this depth arises impulses of intelligence, the same intelligence that keeps the universe and its process in perfect order—this is what is meant by "all knowledge is within." Out of this depth our true identity as Divinity bubbles up to illumine our mind and consciousness. The impulses create a dynamic flow of information we perceive as inspiration and spiritual awareness and eventually appear at the surface as our "enlightened thoughts." Learning to access this depth, to consciously experience this, is the objective of superconscious meditation. Learning to do this will effectively change the outcome of what is occurring in the cellular gaps—we can reset and change the course of the trajectory of the chemical messages within the gaps. This is done by "being" in the gaps between our thoughts.

How to Proceed

1. **Do an Inventory**
   As a practical exercise ask yourself: What thoughts are habitual? i.e., what thoughts or attitudes keep making it across the gap? Worry? Anxiety? Doubt? Fear? Anger? Depression? Pessimism? Resentment? Jealousy? Lack of faith or trust in yourself or life?

2. **Read Through the List of Virtues**
   If any of the virtues listed resonate for you then pick just one (or two at the most) for your practice.

Virtues, Qualities, and Attributes

- Love
- Compassion
- Friendliness
- Joy
- Happiness
- Self-Respect
- Humility
- Self-Confidence
- Perfect Health
- Truthfulness
- Forgiveness
- Courage

- Kindness
- Vitality
- Diligence Harmlessness
- Generosity
- Sincerity
- Initiative
- Resourcefulness
- Self-Control
- Reliability
- Service
- Selflessness

- Common Sense
- Determination
- Honesty
- Strength
- Sympathy
- Patience
- Courtesy
- Tolerance
- Self-Reliance
- Poise
- Discipline
- Purity

3. Take the Message into the Gap

Get a mala, or string of prayer beads, usually made with 108 beads (many bookstores carry these). The tradition of 108 beads is open to interpretation—once when Paramahansa Yogananda was asked by one of his students how many rounds of a certain practice to perform, he replied, "Oh, one hundred and eight." When asked why, he said, "It sounds like a good number!"

The best time to practice is at the point in your meditation session when you are experiencing the greatest degree of quiet and stillness (but anytime will suffice). Use your right thumb and right middle finger to grasp the bead next to the beginning bead, and mentally say just the virtue(s) you've chosen from the list. It can be helpful to synchronize the mental repetition with your breath—try it with inhalation or exhalation and see which feels better. Then pause for a brief moment in the silence—this is the gap. Feel as if the quality of the virtue is bubbling up from within you to the surface just as bubbles arise from the depths of a still pond, creating ripples that reverberate throughout the pond. Let it ripple through every cell of your body and through your entire being. Let the "pond" reach stillness again and then move to the next bead and repeat the process. Continue on in this manner for 108 beads.

> Example:
> Grasp a bead and mentally say a chosen virtue, such as, "Happiness." Experience the "ripple" effect, pause, and rest in the stillness for a few seconds. Move to the next bead and again mentally say "Happiness," pause, and rest in the stillness, and so on for 108 repetitions, moving from bead to bead.

Pause momentarily in the gap in between repetitions but for no more than a few seconds, otherwise it will take quite some time to get through 108 repetitions and the mind may begin to wander if given too much time in the gap. One second for the mental repetition of the virtue with a five second pause would make the total time for the 108 beads approximately eleven minutes, which is reasonable for most people. So just do what feels natural and comfortable. When you feel like you have experienced the quality of the particular virtue or just feel ready to move on, reread the list, see what resonates and try others. The evidence of whether or not this practice is working will be in your daily life—are you more aware of the virtue? Is the gap still maintaining habitual patterns or is the virtue now more and more in your awareness?

This practice is not just "positive thinking." It is much more than that. Neither is it reprogramming. When you do this practice on a regular basis you are allowing your Soul qualities to rise to the surface—they are already there, no need to program. The practice is simply a way to consciously access, acknowledge, and open up a way for these virtues to manifest. At the level of the cells of the body, you are giving information to the gaps—creating the chemical equivalent of the chosen virtue. This chemical equivalency will saturate your cells with the positive energy associated with the virtues and unblock those areas that are not in line with the purity of your Soul. Eventually, with diligent practice, old habitual negative patterns and the associated chemistry will be altered.

In summary, it is the simultaneous gap between our thoughts and between our cells where there is a temporary pause. The gap can even be recognized between our breaths—at the point where inhalation pauses and turns into exhalation. The trajectory after the pause can take either a positive or a negative direction depending upon the ramifications of the content of our subconscious mind and the effect of these ramifications on the chemistry (neurotransmitters) within the gaps. Within the pause is divine Presence—a silent connection to the depth of our being—and contains unlimited potential. To grasp this is to grasp the key to breaking free from the past and therefore to changing the future. We can take charge of this by being observant, being present, and being conscious of our thoughts and of the gap. It is a subtle awareness and requires keen perception, but by following all the practices outlined in these sutras the gap becomes more and more accessible.

Brain Sutra 15

—⚇—

A Continuation of Sutra 14, "Get into the Gap"

Did you find the gap? And were you surprised by what you found? Were you able to identify habitual patterns of thought regularly sneaking across the gap?

Did you notice that reactions to things, people, and events around you occur at an unconscious level? It is really not that anything outside of us produces the reactions but rather it is what is happening in these gaps that is the key. In the gaps are all the potential reactions to externals— when we are not conscious of the reactions they are mechanically driven and the chemicals (neurotransmitters) are released in specific proportions relative to our perception and our translation of externals. There are chemicals released when we allow thoughts of fear, anxiety, depression, worry, and doubt just to name a few. There is of course chemistry for love, compassion, awe, kindness, and all the virtues. The brain will create and reinforce pathways too as thoughts and emotions are experienced over and over again. The more we allow a certain thought or emotion to be present the more established the pathway in the brain becomes, just as if you learned to play a musical instrument. Brain imaging shows parts of the brain devoted to playing a musical instrument increase in size, connections, and activity—it is the same way with thoughts we habitually think.

The so-called placebo effect too is the result of what happens in the gap—when we believe in something, when our mind is thoroughly convinced, the chemistry of the gap responds accordingly, and real measurable results occur. It is not a phenomenon, magic, or mystery but rather is the measure of how powerful our mind-body connection really is—sages tell us mind and body are not separate but that the body is an extension of the mind.

The Gap Is Where Health or Disease Begins

Scientific proof of the power of the gap's chemistry has been well documented in the work of Dr. Fuad Lechin of Caracas, Venezuela. Dr. Lechin discovered that many diseases are the result of the cellular gaps whose chemistry has gone awry. He researched and developed an approach to some of the most devastating of all illnesses, including severe autoimmune and certain types of cancer. His approach is to first carefully measure the chemical imbalances at the gaps (neurotransmitters, stress chemicals, and neurohormones) and use this information to design the appropriate adjustments to the gaps chemistry. This is not a blind symptom-based approach but rather uses physiological data along with psychological indexes including depression profiles and "non-coping" reactive stress patterns. The treatment uses short-term inexpensive common pharmacological substances aimed to bring the gaps back to chemical homeostasis. He has proved his methods over decades of research and thousands of case histories time and time again. Dr. Lechin himself, after being diagnosed with myasthenia gravis, applied this approach and within six weeks of treatment (designed to manipulate the neurotransmitters in the gap) he was free of the illness. His classic text, *Neurocircuitry and Neuroautonomic Disorders*, is profound in knowledge and implication. Unfortunately, much of his work has been largely ignored outside Venezuela. This information, however, reinforces the immense importance of the gap and what it can mean to intervene at this level. The various practices outlined in these Brain Sutras can guide us to access our own "inner" pharmacy and direct it accordingly.

As presented in Brain Sutra 14, in the gap between our thoughts lies pure potentiality, a connection to the creative source within, prior to any manifestation—this is the silent field of all possibility. This momentary and largely imperceptible pause between our thoughts is like a car's transmission going into neutral before shifting gears. This pause correlates with the body's pause between communication networks, the chemistry in the gaps between the cells sending and receiving messages. The chemistry will express as the molecules of emotion depending on the thoughts that produce the activating or inhibiting messages across the gap. In pause mode the gap is in neutral—the same potential exists here between the cells that exists between our thoughts. If we can learn to recognize these gaps and intervene at these subtle moments we literally have the opportunity to *break habitual patterns*.

The "habitual patterns" used in this context refers to all the subconscious conditionings that form our ego identity and motivate our actions and reactions. At the core we are unconditioned spiritual being, but as we express through mind and body our thoughts and emotions manifest correlating to our individual chemistry.

Among persons experiencing addiction a common slang phrase is, "I have a bad habit," meaning they have a significant addiction. The words "habit" and "addiction" used in this way refer to the same thing. This also applies to our own individual chemistry in the sense that not only is the experience of "ego identity" a habit, but also an internal addiction to our own chemistry. In other words we will tend to support those relationships, thoughts, emotions, beliefs and attitudes, whether they are in our best interest or not, as if we are addicted to them. This is because our individual chemistry defines us, supports us and is the sense of who we are. We therefore, strive to maintain the chemistry of our ego identity because without it we have no reference point for this definition of who we are.

Have you ever wondered why a certain attitude, behavior, or relationship cannot be overcome even when we clearly know better and we know it is not serving us? Do we tend to just chalk it up to bad karma, past lives or challenging astrological influences? No, it is simply due to chemistry. When we worry, or when we are fearful or anxious, we have a certain chemistry.

When we are in love we have a specific chemistry. When we are angry or depressed we have corresponding chemistry. What we experience as love is in Reality the strong internal chemistry we have associated with the person we are "in love with." It is the chemistry and the association with the person that makes us choose them as the object of our "love." A parent "bonds" with their child due to the chemistry of oxytocin (a bonding chemical). When we are repelled by a person or thing, too, this is a chemical reaction driving us. We see this manifest on large cultural scales as well—the perception of "that person is different from me," is chemistry and can go back generations, leading to racism, religious intolerance, even resulting in genocide.

We must be on guard too when we engage with people whose words we accept as authority on any given subject because just as there is the "placebo effect" there is a "nocebo effect" as well. Nocebo is defined as that which creates a harmful effect. Therefore, a negative comment, diagnosis or prediction from a person we view as "expert" can have a deleterious effect on the chemistry of our gaps and produce a harmful effect in itself.

> The chemicals composing the average size human body are worth approximately $160.00!
>
> DATAGENETICS

Does this mean our thoughts and emotions are reduced to being just a menagerie of chemicals and electrochemical reactions? The answer is yes. But that is not to take anything away from the joys, romances, wonder, and poetry of life, human dynamics, dramas, or anything else of our amazing experience of this world. This dance of the "molecules of emotion" is a dance orchestrated and choreographed by chemistry. However, we do not want to miss the ultimate goal of our human experience—and that is to eventually wake up to our spiritual identity beyond the chemistry. This can be accomplished by applying enlightened information as we understand that we do not have to be at the mercy of the chemistry of our bodies. We can use "consciousness technologies" to first observe what is happening and then secondly to change the outcome in the gap.

The spiritual path is just as it says: it is a trail where we end up discovering our real identity. We are unconditioned consciousness (spirit) and with this awareness we can learn to work with the mind-body's chemistry, correct it, and dissolve the habits and conditionings.

The tools we have been given are spiritual technologies and are used for this purpose. Throughout these fifteen sutras the main points and practices have been delineated. The methods are fairly simple but do require diligent practice, patience, and time to see results—results are guaranteed though, some sooner, some later (and some instantaneous).

In summary from the previous Brain Sutras:

1. Practice being conscious-awake and present.
2. Make your subconscious transparent.
3. Practice superconscious meditation.
4. Learn to observe the gaps.

5. Intervene at the gap when you identify a problematic thought, emotion, or pattern.
6. Practice the "virtue" repetition exercise described in Brain Sutra 14.

Brain Sutra 16

—⚇—

Merging Science and Mysticism

Do unto others as you would have them do unto you.
The Golden Rule

Why is there a timeless universal acknowledgment of the profound truth as stated in the Golden Rule? Most people resonate with this statement and recognize its deep significance. In various ways references to this run through the world religions:

Christianity
Judge not, that ye be not judged...
Matthew 7:1

Confucianism
Do not do to others what you would not like yourself. Then there will be no resentment against you, either in the family or in the state.
Analects 12:2

Buddhism
Hurt not others in ways that you yourself would find hurtful.
Udana-Varga 5,1

Hinduism
This is the sum of duty; do naught unto others what you would not have them do unto you.
MAHABHARATA 5,1517

Islam
No one of you is a believer until he desires for his brother that which he desires for himself.
SUNNAH

Judaism
What is hateful to you, do not do to your fellowman. This is the entire Law; all the rest is commentary.
TALMUD, SHABBAT 31D

Taoism
Regard your neighbor's gain as your gain, and your neighbor's loss as your own loss.
TAI SHANG KAN YIN P'IEN

Zoroastrianism
That nature alone is good which refrains from doing another whatsoever is not good for itself.
DADISTEN-I-DINIK, 94,5

This is more than a moral or ethical principle of reciprocity: it is an unfailing law.

There are several layers to understanding the karmic principle, from the mundane to the mystical.

At a basic level, following this law provides stability and harmony when a culture holds this truth as a goal. If not, then we see societies where "I, me, mine" becomes the mantra and "every man for himself" is the guiding principle. The consequence of this type of thinking is always the same: self-serving, eventually leading to greed, manipulation and oppression, the downfall of a balanced and caring society.

Aside from the fundamental karmic fact of "as ye sow, so shall ye reap," there is a more profound and significant basis here. Science and mysticism are merging and giving us clues now to what is really happening in, and as, the world we live in.

In the book *Super Brain*, Professor Rudolf Tanzi of Harvard Medical School writes: "Countless top scientists have now concluded, it is consciousness that creates matter, not the other way around."

In fact, matter is not matter at all, but waves, and these waves are consciousness—intelligence!

And…from French physicist Bernard d'Espagnat: "The doctrine that the world is made up of objects whose existence is independent of human consciousness turns out to be in conflict with the facts established by experiment."

Science is now confirming the message of enlightened seers, saints, and sages—this world is not as it appears to our unawakened senses. And it is possible to awaken our spiritual senses and see through to Reality, but a laboratory is not necessary—the real laboratory is in our own consciousness, accessible through meditative disciplines. For when we awake we apprehend the interconnectedness of everything; we understand the enigmatic statement expounded in the Vedas thousands of years ago, "Seeing, the seer and that which is seen are one."

We then grasp the real meaning of the Golden Rule. Following the Golden Rule is in essence putting into practice the fundamental merger of science and mysticism: what appears as "other": people, things, externals, is, in truth, *you*. It is all your innermost consciousness appearing to be different and separate from you. We are fooled by our "separate" physical bodies and seeing the world through our physical eyes. We falsely interpret this and believe we are confined and localized to our bodies and that our identity lies within these bodies. We identify with the body and appear to live "in them" and everything and everyone is "out there." Yes, these physical bodies are our vehicles, temples, and serve as our reference point in this world, but enlightened mystics (and now science) tell us something that is difficult to believe, and almost incomprehensible to our limited view. The lofty mystical statements that sometimes sound cliché, make some of us wince or at least seem way over our head, now have a real practical application and Reality. The real meaning of the golden rule, therefore, pertains to the Reality of our existence—what we call "others" is not entirely accurate. What you "do unto others" you are in truth doing to yourself. We are playing what appears to be separate parts. But in truth, in the essence of our being, we are one Divine Self playing all the roles.

The ego self, the personality or the sense of individuality, does not particularly like this—it is the primary obstacle to Self-realization. In Sanskrit it is called Ahamkara:

> Ahamkara—the making of the limited egoic self or "I" with its twin delusions of ownership and agency. That which makes us think of ourselves as (a) independent "subjects" of consciousness whose awareness is "our own" private property rather than a portion of the universal or Divine awareness and (b) makes us believe that our ego or "I" is an independent subject or agent of action separate and apart from action, rather than a part of the power of action immanent with the Divine awareness.

The "I, me, mine" objects to the dissolution (crucifixion) of what is perceived as individual identity/ego. This is the illusion though; the personality-ego is a transitory and temporary reference point, built by culture, education, and the storehouse of memory. We always have been and always will be one with divine Being; we are not the ego, we are not the mind, we are not the body. This awareness and its realization puts us to the test because we can no longer hold the same notions of life, the world and success. Name, fame, ego, wealth, power all melt away under the light of truth here. We are not here to serve ego, but to serve our larger real Self, and kindness to all, service to all, respect to all, is the culmination of the realization of one-ness.

Humility is then the natural state, not a goal because nothing is higher or lower, no one better or worse, no one more and no one less "God," and this pertains to the animal kingdom as well. Ancient Vedic scriptures say that the dawning of the next enlightened age will be evidenced by two things: 1. Human will stop killing human, 2. Humans will stop killing our companion beings on this planet (animals).

Brain Sutra 17

Making It Real

As we progress along the spiritual path at times the eternal truths can seem otherworldly or idealistic. People who claim to be atheist or agnostic often view with skepticism the inconsistency of religion and the behavior of those claiming to be spiritual. The world at this time in history is experiencing great struggles as the obvious problems in our culture and society are identified and become less and less acceptable to more and more people. According to Vedic time cycle calculations, we are just a few hundred years out of the collective inertia of a dark age. However, we are now in an ascending cycle where the light of truth, understanding and progress will only increase exponentially. We will see dramatic positive changes over the decades to come—struggle too, but the immense universal drive in the direction of evolution is unfailing and as individuals awaken, our world will experience ever-increasing harmony.

As explained in Brain Sutra 8, this is still a time cycle of conflict and we are just at the beginning but if there were no struggle, nothing would change. When we hear almost every day of the tragedies and calamities, the obvious political, social, environmental, religious, and economic challenges, we can lose hope. We can get frustrated, pessimistic, frightened and foster attitudes that actually contribute to the inertia of ignorance. We all experience personal tragedies as well—some experience devastating circumstances and events that make us ask, "How could a God let this happen?" The instinctive reaction to the problems we face is fear and contraction. If the great saints and sages tell us, "All this is God!" how are we to reconcile this with what we are faced with every day? How do we make this awareness real? How do we apply this? These truths all sound nice but for some of us they may remain radical, fantasy, too idealistic, at a distance and difficult to comprehend.

The weight of Maya is a strong influence (Maya: the veil or the illusion of duality: the perception that God does not exist or is some far-off thing rather than the pure silent ever-presence it is). There are almost seven billion humans on the planet now and science and mystics tells us that although we are separated by our physical bodies, our minds are not as individual as we would like to believe. According to the time cycles of evolution, the majority of the almost seven billion humans are not yet awake-enlightened. This creates a collective mind inertia that is enormous especially when we try to adhere to, and to put into practice, the great teachings that go against the collective thought. The world of seeming opposites makes it very difficult for us to see through to the source, God. The more "in the world" we are the greater the challenge. An inner world must be developed—instilled with an inner peace that is detached from what is happening externally.

There are of course individuals who remove themselves from the world to avoid the discord and the distractions in order seek spiritual realities. There are those who decide to devote their lives to solitude and lives of quiet service, and this too has an impact on the collective mind of humanity. And then there are those peaceful-warrior Souls like Mahatma Gandhi, Martin Luther King Jr., and many others who while firmly grounded in unshakable truth consciousness, take on the enormous task of challenging the untruths. We can arrange our lives so that we see to our spiritual awareness and play our part in no less a way. If you have somehow found these writings and are reading this now, this is in fact, essential. You are being called upon, not by these words, but by your own inner being to "make it real." This does not mean that we all have to go out and be activists for world change. We can if we feel so led. It is not necessary either, to retire from the world and the worlds discord in order to be enlightened. Our silent "knowing" the truth has a significant impact and influence on the collective consciousness of humanity and is a great blessing.

The challenge is simply this: "Reality" cannot be grasped intellectually with the mind. We can think about it, we can contemplate it, but that is not the same as the experience of it. Words cannot describe it. To be "realized," it must be experienced—it is not a thought—it is "That" which is awareness itself. This experience is not at a distance and not to be searched for. It is always present; it is the "you of you" and has always been and always will be. If we search we are like a fish in the middle of the ocean searching for water! Awakening to this can be a spontaneous event but more often than not, a systematic program of spiritual practice is required to gradually refine and transform awareness so that the truth is revealed.

Science and mysticism agree that consciousness is all there is, and whether or not we are aware of this, we can accept this fact. Then we can strive to always be conscious-present and to no longer allow ourselves to be fooled by our sense of individuality/separation and fooled by the belief in the individuality of others. We can remind ourselves to view the world from the perspective of absolute consciousness in, and as, all things. This is nondual perception versus perception of duality: "Where there is two (duality), there is fear." The shift of awareness from duality to nonduality is a great blessing and *is* the dissolution of fear. There is no longer any such thing as accident or anything evil or anything "out there" out to do us harm or throw obstacles in the way of our highest awareness. Everything, every event, is here for our enlightenment when we realize the consciousness of oneness.

Patanjali, the codifier of the Yoga Sutras, stated that to awaken we must surrender our "sense of separation" from Divinity. It is just a false "sense," and not real, and therefore, it can be immediately let go of—a simple shift in perspective. When this is done, and we have the real experience, the whole world appears anew—this is the real meaning of being born again. As we do this it is as if we are realigning the mind, piece by piece. The mind has many, many compartments and each time we realize truth, each time we realize that we are Divinity at our core, we penetrate and affect another area of the mind until eventually over time, the whole of the mind is transformed. The primary tools we use for this are superconscious meditation and the practice of being conscious-present described in detail in these sutras.

Try this exercise at the end of your next meditation session:

Look upon everyone you know or have contact with, simply and purely as divine Being. Then expand this awareness to include everything in your life, to all the world, to all living things, to all Souls everywhere, the planets, the universes and infinite space. As often as you can, at intervals during your day, and if you awaken during the night, remind yourself of the truth.

> See the world as your Self Have faith in the way things are Love the world as your Self
> Then you can care for all things.
>
> TAO TE CHING

Brain Sutra 18

Think in the Gap

The conscious mind is driven by the subconscious mind and creates boundaries and opposites: me versus you, us versus them, my country/race/religion/team/political party versus yours. This automatic perception is fostered by the brain's intricate information and memory stores creating our sense of individuality, sense of separation and definition of self. In the gap we have the opportunity to catch hold of these automatic divisions the mind projects, and if we so choose, we can change them.

Why should we do this? Because this automatic process is the root of discord from a personal to a global scale. Almost every problem and challenge we see can be traced back to this. Are we to think a utopian existence is even possible, where we see cooperation and harmony? Or is it wiser to remain cynical, believing that there are greedy, self-serving individuals who will take advantage if we are not careful. This is a crucial question that we can only answer individually according to our own understanding.

In the fall/winter of 2015, two movies will debut: the first is a dramatization of the housing loan failure in '08 that the banks essentially knew was coming, and many profited from, leading to the collapse of the world economy. The second is about the MD who sought to educate the public regarding the devastating aftereffects of multiple head trauma experienced by football players.

This led to the eventual exposure of the NFL's prior knowledge of the damage done to the player's brains and the attempts to cover it up. Rather than getting angry at the banks, politicians, and corporations, we can appreciate and acknowledge the consciousness that is exposing these deceptions. The mind-set at the root of the deceptions come from brains whose programming has "I-me-mine" priorities. But the mind-set that is exposing these deceptions is one that can change things—it is a consciousness of "waking up."

We must be sensible, practical, as informed as possible and see to our welfare and the welfare of those around us. At the same time we can see to our enlightened inner consciousness—we can work with our inner awareness. The collective mind of humanity is influenced by our individual awareness and our thoughts, therefore cultivating our own depth of knowing can be one of the most important contributions to the uplifting of world consciousness.

If you have been practicing the gap exercise described in sutras 14/15, then you may have noticed the gap between thoughts—the pause when you are conscious-present and the possibilities therein. With continued practice the automatic and unconscious reaction patterns are neutralized and the trajectory of non-useful thoughts and emotions redirected. This produces not only a change in thinking and behavior but the corresponding change in the chemistry of the brain and body. As we become more conscious we can introduce questions to ourselves in the gap. These questions can give our decisions and interactions positive direction as we interject them into the pause.

A useful and easy-to-remember tool for inner questioning is often seen posted on social media as well as in inspirational literature. It is the acronym THINK (True, Helpful, Inspirational, Necessary, Kind) and is very appropriate for the gap. When we become conscious of the gap between thoughts we have the opportunity to really "think" and not just to react. This exercise is used for our personal interactions with others and gives us the opportunity to practice being conscious and aware through communication. We use the acronym to remind us to ask ourselves if we are being guided by each respective item as we interact with others.

T is for true.

Ask yourself, "Is what I am about to say true?" Perhaps at times it is just a matter of qualifying what we are saying, such as, "in my opinion…" But other times we must look at the source of information we have accepted and determine if the source is in fact correct. Oftentimes information we have accepted as "facts" are just other people's opinions and not necessarily true. There are facts and then there are opinions. Learning to distinguish between the two can be all that is necessary.

H is for helpful.

Ask yourself, "Is what I am about to say helpful?" Sometimes we can say too much. We can inadvertently subvert another person's learning process by giving them directions or answers to questions they could benefit by learning themselves. At other times what we might intend as constructive criticism is taken as a dig or damaging to another's self-worth.

I is for inspirational.

Ask yourself, "Is what I am about to say inspirational?" Every day, at least one time, make it a conscious practice to uplift, encourage, and inspire someone by telling them how much you sincerely appreciate them—anyone from the checkout person, to a loved one, fellow workers, or to random people you meet.

Also, without being pretentious or condescending, it can be a great gift to thank someone for teaching you how to be patient and tolerant especially if you do it with sincere gratitude. Both of you benefit.

N is for necessary.

Ask yourself, "Is what I am about to say necessary?" Sometimes we may react out of our own anger, our own sense of "how things should be," or a sense of violation, and this does not do any good and can end up being hurtful to another and actually create resistance. Sometimes it is better to just be quiet and to let others gain their own insight and awareness if indeed there is a transgression.

K is for kind.

Ask yourself, "Is what I am about to say kind?" Kindness should be the guiding compass for all we say and do. Kindness expressed goes on exponentially. It is contagious and it is not an exaggeration to say it changes lives. We do not know the downstream effects of our simple acts of kindness—it can be monumental.

Life Is Our Spiritual Practice

The lives we live, each and every interaction we have, is the test and opportunity for our spiritual growth and practice. The gap affords us a momentary pause, an opportunity to wake up and to change repetitive unconscious patterns and to ultimately fulfill our purpose for being here. As you use this acronym, over time you will no longer need to go through and remember each item, they will be consolidated as a whole into a natural guiding principle for all your interaction.

Brain Sutra 19

Our Natural State

The four states of consciousness as delineated in enlightenment teachings are deep dreamless sleep, dreaming sleep, conscious wakefulness, and the fourth state called superconsciousness. Superconsciousness is always present and is the silent witness to the other three states.

Superconsciousness is defined as: the mind of light, the all-knowing intelligence of the Soul. At its deepest level, the superconscious is the Divine Mind of God. The superconscious mind works through the conscious and subconscious states and is the source of intuition, clarity, and insight. It is always there; it is the source of our very existence.

The goal of spiritual practice is to live in the superconscious state by learning to consciously access it through meditation and being conscious-present (being in the "gap"). We can learn to recognize it in our moment-to-moment awareness; it is our natural state.

The late Satguru Sivaya Subramuniyaswami, in his book, *Merging with Siva* (Siva is the all- pervading absolute Divine consciousness), writes about superconsciousness:

When are you superconscious? It is easier to know when you are not superconscious than when you are superconscious, because your superconsciousness is such a natural state. It is such a beautiful state. It is such a full, wholesome state to be in, that you are not aware generally that you are superconscious. When you are not feeling too well within yourself, you are not superconscious. When you are feeling really good and satisfied with yourself, you are superconscious. When your timing is right, when everything is happening right during the day, you are superconscious. When nothing seems to be happening right, then your awareness is flowing through one of the congested areas of the thought realm. When everything seems to be going wrong, you are flowing through the instinctive area or a congested intellectual area. When you are arguing with yourself, you are not superconscious. You are flowing through an area of the intellectual mind, taking two points of view and flowing from one to another. When discussing something with someone, you are not superconscious, for superconsciousness is a one-way street. You speak right from the core of existence without really thinking about what you are going to say. You just speak out and hear what you said afterwards. When you are arguing with someone, you are not superconscious. You have moved into a congested area of the thought strata of the mind and you are verbalizing it, and are congesting the aura too. Then awareness has to be unwound from that area of the mind and directed back to superconsciousness. When you are disturbed about yesterday, or even conscious that there was a yesterday, you are not in a superconscious state. When you are afraid, you are not in a superconscious state. When you are peaceful, when you are calm, when you are in the eternity of the moment, when you feel secure on the inside of you, you are in a superconscious state.

Superconsciousness is not something you will get, because you have never been without it. You are superconscious this very minute."

As we develop our understanding of when we are and when we are not actively and consciously manifesting the superconscious, we realize it is basically a choice. We can choose to be present and open, and flow with life. We can choose to stop worrying and being afraid. We can choose to stop arguing with, and/or judging, ourselves and others.

Cultivating superconscious awareness is done first through learning to observe ourselves, working with any negative thinking or programming we identify in the "gap," and then make a conscious choice to stop and change the negative flow of thinking/behaving.

There are certain times when the background of congested thoughts in the intellectual and instinctive areas of the mind can be observed. The first is during the night, if we find our sleep is disturbed or we find ourselves waking often. The second is when we awake in the morning. The subconscious mind is closer to the surface at these times and its contents more visible. If you have occasional nights when your mind is trying to solve a problem or a worry, if you have disturbing dreams, or if you wake up with some vague (or not-so-vague) anxiety, try this:

1. Do not try to analyze or solve the problem.
2. Prepare a simple "mantra," a word or a phrase that is representative of how you want to think or feel according to when you are superconscious. For guidance on this refer to the excerpt from above: "When you are peaceful, when you are calm, when you are in the eternity of the moment, when you feel secure on the inside of you, you are in a superconscious state."

3. Use the "gap" exercise described in Brain Sutra 14 and practice your "mantra" or choose a virtue from the list. Then, immediately (or as soon as you remember to) upon awakening, mentally repeat your mantra with slow rhythmic diaphragmatic breathing. If habitual or intrusive thoughts persist, just keep redirecting your awareness back to your mantra and back to your breath. If you are sleepy, your mind may wander off, but again, gently keep pulling it back to your mantra. Over time the positive superconscious conviction of the mantra will become firmly established and impressed in all levels of your mind.

With persistence over time you will notice that when you wake up, your mantra is right there with you. You may also notice that during your day it is right there with you too. In effect you are reeducating the subconscious and all levels of the mind.

The tone and content of our dreams and nighttime musings mirror the stability and harmony of our subconscious and will reflect in our daily lives. When sleep and dreams are disturbed it is because our subconscious is trying to work out conflicts and our daily lives will express the inner conflict in the form of external problems and issues. Many of us repress uncomfortable memories that, when unresolved, lurk in the background and can create current problems in various areas of our lives. Everything that has happened to us is stored in the subconscious.

There is recent research from Emory University School of Medicine showing that the memory of trauma experienced by our ancestors can be passed down, literally by being programmed into the DNA. According to the research, events will trigger the inherited DNA reaction pattern programming. If our parents or grandparents, or beyond, went through traumatic periods or events in their lives we may inherit certain characteristics as a result. This can include fear, anxiety, worry, anger, and depression reaction patterns to name a few. Perhaps this is why we see generational trauma and collective grieving patterns, and patterns of racial and ethnic conflict, among so many peoples that have been going on for hundreds or thousands of years—the memories are inherited and passed on to subsequent generations. Nevertheless, we are responsible for how we respond to life now and we can eliminate and neutralize the subconscious conflicts and programming with the method outlined above. Evidence suggests the DNA programming is indeed altered in this way. Enlightenment teachings tell us that when we awaken to superconsciousness, seven generations before us and seven generations after us are blessed by our awakening. Perhaps this has a direct connection with the new discoveries about DNA.

When we clear the subconscious of conflict and thereby allow the superconscious mind to shine forth unimpeded, sleep and dreams will be blissful, and our daily life will be a blissful flow of perfect timing and Divine order as an expression.

Brain Sutra 20

Nature or Nurture?

From our genetic blueprint (DNA) we inherit certain physical as well as psychological characteristics. Male or female, skin color, eye color, hair color, body type, and the propensity for certain diseases are among the physical traits. Psychologically we know now that we inherent fear patterns and fear responses that can reach back several generations. Many studies over the past few decades show even more startling data. One pair of twins, separated at four weeks of age, raised separately, and then reunited at the age of thirty-nine, found they both suffered from tension headaches, smoked Salem cigarettes, were prone to nail-biting, drove the same type of car and even vacationed at the same beach in Florida! Even religiosity was identified as a genetic trait in another study. The scientific consensus now is that the nature versus nurture roles are about 50/50 in terms of influencing psychological development, although this research is still ongoing. That means we inherit 50 percent of our psychological makeup from our ancestors, their DNA, and the other 50 percent of our makeup is from environmental influences. These influences include our culture, family, friends, media, teachers and all the societal influences we have around us. And these influences, not being from our genetics, begin to condition and create new DNA information that is passed on. This raises the questions: Are we at the mercy of our DNA? Are we at the mercy of the environment that imposes conditioning upon us? Or can we alter our own DNA by becoming more spiritually conscious, identifying the nonuseful tendencies, extinguish them and thereby change and eliminate the nonuseful tendencies. Can we actually eliminate the risk of passing on negative conditioning? It is possible... enlightenment teachings have been saying this for hundreds of years. When we work on our own conditioning we are changing our DNA, repairing as well as stopping the karmic cycles of conditioned responses.

Understanding how this information applies to the spiritual path can be useful and can help us identify our conditionings: how, what, and why we think, feel, and behave—why we do the things we do.

In effect what we get from our ancestors (nature), and what we get from our environment (nurture) have equal weight. This explains our inherited, as well as environmentally created, individual conditioning. Just as software is programmed, literally the brain and body's imprinting of electrochemical information in the DNA determines our propensities, likes, and dislikes in life. Because the negative conditioning is what we struggle against if our goal is to wake up, then learning how to navigate through this is crucial.

Stop now and ask yourself:

The three traits I most admire about my mother (or the person who raised me) are

    1.
    2.
    3.

The three traits I admire about my father

    1.
    2.
    3.

The three traits I do not admire about my mother
1.
2.
3.

The three traits I do not like about my father
1.
2.
3.

As you review your responses be completely honest with yourself. Remember there is a 50 percent probability you have inherited these same traits; both the negative and the positive. Many times as we mature and recognize the negative traits in our parents we learn to recognize the tendencies within our own makeup, we resolve many of the issues just by seeing them. If there is a negative trait you identified that is still present for you, this is something to be recognized and to work on. This is a conditioning that can be eradicated but to do this requires that you make it a practice to be present, recognize, and be conscious in situations where this pattern emerges.

The brain's autopilot is what we most have to struggle with because it keeps us in habitual ways of thinking and reacting, requiring little if any conscious presence.

Brain Sutra 21

—∽∽—

Our Bodies Are Keeping Score

Every experience we have leaves a trace upon us. In a very real way, the body keeps score. This score is like a tally of various experiences, both positive and negative. Most of us know someone who shows the signs (the score) of the negative effects of stress. Abraham Lincoln is said to have remarked, "Every man over forty is responsible for his face."[4] Each experience shapes the physiology of our body—negative experiences take a toll as the score ads up as well as the positive experiences. It is up to us to be aware of this and to use our experiences for learning the lessons necessary for our growth.

The traces left by experience are electrochemical patterns imprinted in the brain/body. Negative experiences such as trauma do not necessarily have to be the source of all the imprints. There are of course significant traumatic experiences that create deep wounds but there are also seemingly harmless events that create equally strong impressions that can have a domino effect throughout our lives. We may blame our current feelings and reactions on people or

---

4 https://archive.org/stream/abrahamlincolnqulinc_17/abrahamlincoln-qulinc_17_djvu.txt

circumstances in the present as the source. But the truth is we may just be juxtaposing feelings from former events on to our current experience.

Do you have particular negative behavior patterns in relationships with loved ones, friends, or anyone else that keep recurring? Do you ever find yourself saying, "Why does this always happen to me? What am I not getting here?" Do you feel uncomfortable around certain types of people or places? Do you have fears or phobias? Do you startle easily? Do you have insomnia? Do you have to stay "busy" all the time? Are you lacking or struggling in any area of your life? Do you have chronic physical issues that clearly are exacerbated by stress? Addictions? Do you have to search for your true feelings, do you feel out-of-touch at times? This can all be the result of an accumulation of responses to past experience that is being triggered, repeated, "blamed" on, and attached to current circumstances, people, or events. This is not to blame the past but rather to identify the current issues and see the connection with the past. This enables us to break the cycle—it makes it conscious.

Ram Dass said, "If you think you are enlightened, go spend a week with your family!"[**5] Not only do we get pulled into virtually all the conditioned patterns developed over our lives when we are with the people who were around us during our crucial developmental years, but the people who we knew at the various stages project all their notions and opinions about us on us as well! This can be very unsettling—our voices may change, we may regress and feel like children, we may feel old behaviors and self-conscious beliefs about ourselves emerging. These family get-togethers can be a great opportunity to observe the "acting out" of patterns!

---

5 [**] https://www.ramdass.org/ram-dass-quotes/

Do Not Blame Past Lives

According to enlightenment teachers, our experience now is the carryover from past lives—our lessons continue on until we have resolved them all, realizing life's ultimate purpose and finally experiencing liberation of consciousness. The effect from the past is the cause of the present and if not resolved will keep creating the same effect-cause-effect-cause cycle over and over. When we learn the lessons and make the appropriate adjustments, we consciously eliminate the negative effects and introduce new positive causes. It is in the "here and now" that we have the ability to respond (response-ability) to repetitive patterns (karma). Looking for past life sources can be nothing more than a distraction from dealing with the "here and now."

The Body Remembers

When we recall a past negative event in our life, if it is unresolved, we will experience a similar body chemistry to the original event because we remember the incident no matter how long in the past it occurred. If we feel sadness, hopelessness, regret, guilt, anger, shame, remorse, or any uncomfortable emotion then it is likely the memory and emotion associated with it has not been resolved. When we recall a positive experience, the same applies: the positive chemistry can be intentionally brought about. There is a growing awareness in the therapeutic community that along with other appropriate interventions, body-centered approaches to healing trauma and stress responses are essential. The body keeps score and takes on stress and emotional patterns (chemistry) that reflect the stress in the form of poor breathing patterns, muscle tension/stress patterns, gastrointestinal reactions, autoimmune illness, aches and pains. These body patterns can be released by using breath combined with body awareness practices.

There are however, individual differences and needs for different psychological makeups that should be taken into account before one engages in a meditative practice. A recent study reported that 7.9 percent of people who try meditation or some form of contemplative practice have a negative experience. There is even a growing movement called "The Dark Night Project"[6] that looks at the negative experiences that occur with this percentage of people who try contemplative or meditative practices. It is notable too, however, that a 2010 paper published in *American Psychologist* points to dramatic instances where psychotherapy has caused serious harm to a patient.

---

6 * The Dark Night Project name is taken from the title of the classic mystical text, *Dark Night of the Soul*, written by the sixteenth-century Carmelite monk Saint John of the Cross. Unfortunately, the Dark Night Project dwells almost entirely on the "darkness" and leaves out the very purpose and explanation for the process of moving through the "darkness"—the culmination of which leads to the deepest Soul awakening as described by St. John:

> This enkindling and yearning of love are not always perceived by the soul. For in the beginning, when the spiritual purgation commences, all this Divine fire is used in drying up and making ready the wood (which is the soul) rather than in giving it heat. But, as time goes on, the fire begins to give heat
> to the soul, and the soul then very commonly feels this enkindling heat of love. Further, as the understanding is being more and more purged by means of this darkness, it sometimes comes to pass that this mystical and loving theology,
> as well as enkindling the will, strikes and illumines the other faculty also—that of the understanding—with a certain Divine light and knowledge, so delectably and delicately that it aids the will to conceive a marvelous fervor, and, without
> any action of its own, there burns in it this Divine fire of love, in living flames, so that it now appears to the soul a living fire by reason of the living understanding which is given to it.

To be clear though, not all negative experiences as a result of meditative and contemplative practices are part of the same category. Some are actually desirable and intended as one moves through different levels of the mind—they can serve as a way to identify, desensitize, integrate, neutralize and thereby resolve internal conflict—in effect peeling away the layers that obscure the purity of the Soul. But some of the negative experiences are perhaps caused by premature opening and a misunderstanding of the proper procedure for persons who have deeper unresolved conflicts and/or a history of traumatic experience.

Why are there negative experiences if meditation is supposed to turn on the "relaxation response," make us calm and more focused? Why do some people just give up on meditation?

If there are unresolved issues or trauma, it is not necessarily a conscious memory. In some cases it is just below conscious awareness, lurking in the background as a vague (or not so vague) anxiety or uncomfortable feeling. For example if one was raised in an environment where there was discord and unpredictable behaviors from family, acquaintances, or friends, then this can trigger parts of the brain to either learn to disassociate from the stressful environment and feelings or to be hypervigilant to avoid potential threats in the future. Disassociation has a wide range of severity but essentially it is a defense mechanism—a detachment from the environment and/or from one's own feelings and thoughts—this is the "freeze" response. Hypervigilance manifests as always being on guard as a defense to the unpredictable—always ready for "fight or flight." In the EEG (the electrical activity of the brain: brain waves) you can see the difference: dissociative patterns will show an excess of theta waves and sometimes alpha waves as these people's brains have learned to go "offline" on occasion to avoid negative feelings. The difficult thing about this is these people may not even know that they do this since they sort of disappear by tuning out. The other pattern will show an excess of high beta wave activity which is an indication of extreme over activity as the brain maintains the state of hypervigilance.

Dissociation usually tends toward depression while the hypervigilant is likely to experience anxiety, over-arousal, and other agitated conditions.

We all develop different ways to manage stress. To avoid (or disassociate from) negative feelings some people will engage in almost constant activity, keeping themselves incessantly busy or constantly talking. Some will resort to comfort eating, drugs, and/or alcohol as a way to self-medicate. With the aforementioned 7.9 percent who try meditation, mindfulness or some other form of relaxation training, the repressed memories and/or feelings may begin to emerge. Sometimes the memories are conscious but many will not have the memory of a specific event but rather will have the nonverbal memory in the form of a physical symptom like a headache, disorientation, dizziness, GI upset, insomnia; some will have an emotion of fear, sadness, anxiety, or panic. Some will experience sweating or body shaking, or other uncomfortable feelings associated with the stressful event. These people should not begin with types of meditation or relaxation where one has to keep the body still—this only deepens the uncomfortable feelings and can create (or make one recall) feelings of being "trapped." This is crucial to the deeper healing of the aftereffects of the trauma and these uncomfortable responses and reactions are indications that a different approach is indicated. Professional counseling by someone trained in trauma recovery is important. Moving forms of meditation can also be beneficial—getting the stress patterns out of the body and thereby releasing the pent-up emotion/memory. Some of these include tai chi, qi gong, and hatha yoga. These are movement- oriented practices that use breath combined with body awareness to decongest stagnant energy in the body, release frozen emotion, relax muscle patterns, reduce stress, boost the immune system and many other benefits.

Subramuniyaswami advised that people prone to anger or violence should not try to do sitting forms of meditation or contemplative practices at first. It is advisable for these people to practice karma yoga (learn to perform self-less service for the good of others without attachment to, or expectation of, reward) and/or bhakti yoga (devotional forms of practice where one surrenders one's self to a higher power). Fear and instinctual drives fuel egotism, anger, and violence.

Eventually as one learns to cultivate compassion, empathy, and humility the negative patterns will be extinguished and meditation practice can ensue.

Find Your Breath

One of the simplest and most efficient methods to neutralize negative programming and reaction patterns is to shift awareness to the breath. With awareness on the breath, breathe from the belly, smooth out the breath, eliminate any pausing. With practice, the chemical patterns will change relative to the breath. Breath and mind are intimately connected. The breathing pattern will reflect the content of thought and emotion: i.e., if there is disturbance in the mind there will be disturbed breathing. Breathing patterns will be irregular; some people actually hold their breath, and there is also something called hyperventilation syndrome where panic creates excessive breathing resulting in dizziness and confusion. By using conscious breath awareness the mind can be brought into a less-scattered condition.

> Once an affliction of the mind has been conquered, it cannot return.
>
> THRANGU RIMPOCHE

I recently met with a former convict who was incarcerated nine times in both state and federal prisons over his lifetime. He attributed his "new life," and his successful adjustment to freedom to the two-times-a-week hatha yoga classes he attended while in prison. More specifically to his learning to, in his words, "find my breath." He had a violent childhood, scarred by devastating experiences leaving him with extremely violent reaction patterns—when he was in his "child's mind" he interpreted events according to what life had taught him, that, "violence is the only way to survive." Now, in situations that would have triggered significant violent responses in the past, he found that by just shifting awareness to his breath, he changed the reactions, *permanently*. In his words now, "It was hard a first, but it [breath] saved my life."

Recall the gap exercise in Sutras 14, 15 and 18. If you need to, please reread them. As this former convict learned and as neuroscience tells us, there is one-tenth of a second delay between an outside event and our internal reaction—the one-tenth of a second is the gap. In the one-tenth of a second our brains scan vast memory reserves for "how we should react" based on past experience. If we have negative programming and negative reaction patterns then we will unconsciously react according to those habitual memory patterns—these patterns automatically tell us how we "should" react. Pausing, recognizing the gap, using breath to be present-awake in the one-tenth of a second, is how we can change the unconscious reaction patterns.

Observe-observe-observe

Spend time every day watching for repetitive patterns, for moments when you recognize a familiar annoying feeling. See it as a memory. Observe yourself when you feel frustration, anger, disappointment, or when you feel like a victim, have a disagreement, poor communication or impatience with yourself or others. These are usually indicative of a pattern, of a domino effect of similar situations and incidents from past programming ramifying in the present.

Be conscious of the "score" your body and mind is keeping. Are you tallying up a positive life- affirming, stress-free, prosperous, and spiritually fulfilled scorecard? Or is stress and negativity from old worn-out patterns taking a lead? It is truly up to us once we understand our role. Make a commitment to practice over the next day: *Find your breath and you will find your freedom.*

Recommended Reading

- Bessel van der Kolk, MD. *The Body Keeps the Score: Brain, Mind and Body in the Healing of Trauma.* Viking, 2014.
- Peter A. Levine. *Waking the Tiger: Healing Trauma.* North Atlantic Books, 1997.
- David Emerson and Elizabeth Hopper, PhD. *Overcoming Trauma through Yoga: Reclaiming Your Body.* North Atlantic Books, 2011.

Brain Sutra 22

The Inner Light and the God Spot

> That was the true Light, which lighteth every man that cometh into the world.
>
> JOHN 1:9

Is spiritual awakening and the experience of enlightenment a metaphysical Reality, transcendent, unexplainable, and beyond the physical existence of our brain and body? Or is there a physical correlation, somewhere that is not "other than" these bodies where our enlightenment happens? Some teachings say these bodies are a gift, a microcosm, in "His image," and are necessary vehicles for our incorporeal Souls to awaken to the highest spiritual realization possible.

The common, core mystical experience shared by all religions, all spiritual paths, all mystics, and nearly all people who have an NDE (near-death experience) is the experience of the Divine inner light.

The light is always present in everyone as the root of consciousness; it just needs to be uncovered. In this sense everyone is already enlightened; if there is life, that "life" is Divinity in expression. Animals too, at the core, obviously are this "life" in expression. Therefore as is said over and over again by saints, sages, and seers: the awakening path is simply the revealing of what is already there within! All life is the expression of the one divine Being!

The Great Discovery

In the 1870s, the Liverpool physiologist Richard Canton first identified the spontaneous electrical signals of the living mammalian brain he called "brain waves." It was, however, not until the early nineteenth century that the German psychiatrist and scientist Hans Berger took Canton's discovery further by developing the human electroencephalogram (the EEG). Berger was an avid devotee of the sixteenth-century Dutch philosopher-mystic Spinoza. Spinoza claimed that what is referred to as God is within all life and is the root of all life. Berger was convinced that the EEG rhythms were the expression of the one Divine Reality and that this Divine Reality somehow expressed through the body, pulsating as these waves, giving life to the brain and body. He believed that brain waves are the electrical language, as it were, of the one Divine life, and that they are what makes matter "alive." Unfortunately, his original hypothesis was lost in the "science" of EEG. Nevertheless his discovery of the EEG paved the way for the many present-day technologies used to scan and measure the brain and the various neurological parameters. Indeed, neurofeedback would not be where it is today if it were not for his discovery. We continue to explore the relationship between higher consciousness and its manifestation in the brain.

There is self-knowledge that knows how to heal and regulate the mind-body inherent in consciousness. EEG neurofeedback is a way to reflect consciousness back to itself. This is what is called self-referral and this is what produces healing.

Centuries prior to the discovery of the EEG, and unbeknownst to Berger and his predecessors, yogic science elaborated on the medulla oblongata as the physical "doorway" to the infinite. The Rishis found that the brain stem is the actual physical location where the perception of the Divine inner light occurs. Within the brain stem is the reticular activating system (RAS). The RAS is the regulator of our consciousness—like a pacemaker it activates or deactivates the brain by sending or inhibiting discharges as electrical pulses, brain waves that carry information throughout the rest of the brain and on to the body. The RAS is always "awake" in the background—it has to be—it is conscious in that it is source of the life force and the regulator of all our vital functions that make us "alive": this includes the heartbeat, the cycle of the breath, blood pressure, etc. This explains why at death's doorstep (when the brain stem is shutting down body functions) the inner light is perceived. The brain stem holds the key to the fourth state of consciousness described by seers and in Sanskrit, known as Turiya. Turiya is our "background" state that "witnesses" the other three states: waking, dreaming, and deep-sleep states. The EEG brain wave of Turiya is called delta rhythm: the slowest bandwidth, oscillating between 0 and 4 Hz. For all intents and purposes the higher brain regions of the cortex are "offline" when delta is the dominant rhythm. While in this deepest state, the "I" that is our ego sense of individual identity is dissolved in the universal omnipresent spirit—all sentient beings go into oneness with the Divine consciousness during the delta deep sleep stage whether they know it or not. The RAS is in the so-called "primitive structure" of the brain stem and is known in mystical language as the location for "the mouth of God"—where the omnipresent universal life force enters into the body, individualizes as the Soul, and animates the inanimate flesh. When the life force is withdrawn and the Soul moves on in its journey, the vital functions cease and we call this physical death.

    Certain enlightenment traditions teach techniques, thousands of years old, that are intended to guide the seeker within to the experience of the inner light. Kriya yoga, expounded by Paramahansa

Yogananda in his classic book *Autobiography of a Yogi* is an ancient system, resurrected in the mid-1800s. The methods taught in the kriya yoga system are designed to guide the practitioner to this state of awareness/consciousness. During kriya yoga superconscious meditation, attention is directed to the brain stem by various techniques. The practitioner indeed begins to behold the inner light. In effect we begin to inwardly perceive the emanation, the radiance, of our Soul in the brain stem as it first enters and manifests in the physical plane of existence. By the repeated experience of the perception of the inner light we naturally become increasingly aware of the inherent Divinity and the ensuing "self-revealed" knowledge resident within and carried by the light. The "light that lighteth every man/woman" is the manifestation of superconsciousness in the brain. It is the higher mind, transmitted from the source. This is the knowledge that arises from, and resides, within us all. This inner perception is accompanied by the vibratory hum of creation perceived internally as the sound *Om*. This is what is referred to as "the 'word' made flesh" in John 1:14.

Much more on this to come…

Brain Sutra 23

The Truth Is Simple

The only difference between an enlightened person and an unenlightened person is that the enlightened person knows they are enlightened—the unenlightened person simply does not know it yet. However, at the core, they are both the same: complete, whole, and fully enlightened. This is the simple truth. The one who knows it is not "higher" and the one who does not know it is not "lower."

If anyone believes their enlightenment makes them superior to anyone else, then that is not enlightenment—that is ego. If anyone believes they are enlightened as if they are special and unique, as if they have "attained" something, then this too is ego. Do not bow to anyone out of a notion of superiority, but do bow to everyone acknowledging the same Divinity that resides within. The homeless person scrounging through the trash is just as Divine as the "great master" teaching in the ashram. Never doubt this.

There is no saint, no bodhisattva, no great mystic, no guru, no holy person, no avatar, no "ascended master" and no great yoga master who has attained anything more than you have this very moment. This very existence is enlightenment. We've made a long sojourn to be in these bodies. We are here now and this is our opportunity to wake up to that which we already are and always have been.

The Divine Light that is perceived inwardly in deep meditation at the top of the brain stem, (RAS) mentioned in the last sutra, *is* the manifestation of the One, Pure Consciousness as it comes into expression in the body. Usually this is "seen" with eyes closed as if it were in the center of the brain or at the inside of the forehead. This physical location is considered to be a transdimensional portal— the spiritual eye. The perceived "light" is that which is "life" and therefore is not separate from the divine Source. You are that Light. At this source we are fully in enlightenment. So, you might ask, why is it that we can have so many different experiences?

And, how can some behave so "unenlightened"? The problem is the rest of the brain that is layered on top of this so-called primitive lower brain structure. The layers are the vast neural networks and, just like computer software, get programmed with information, obscuring the Light that is essentially illuminating it. The rest of the brain provides the content but the light we call our consciousness is what is behind the content—and this comes from deep within the brain. We diffuse and differentiate the pure being-ness of the Light as we identify ourselves with the various conditionings (rather than identifying ourselves with the Light). The light from a movie projector is pure, but as the film strip passes before the projected light we see every variety of experience projected on the screen. Our brain stem is like the light of the projector and the rest of the brain is the film strip, coloring our experience with content and conditioning.

> You have to ask yourself the question "Who am I?" This investigation will lead in the end to the discovery of something within you which is beyond the mind. Solve that great problem and you will solve all other problems.
>
> Ramana Maharshi

Brain Sutra 24

—∞—

The Experience of the Inner Light and the Inner Sound

> The Inner Light is the presence of God that lives within us all.
> QUAKERISM

The actual experience of Divinity, God, absolute consciousness, is not a far-off Reality but is an ever-present experience that is available in every moment. Science and many world religions seem to have created a divide between this physical Reality and the world of spiritual truth. To bridge that divide is possible and there is knowledge of the ways and means to make the journey. Many of the spiritual paths, sacred temples, spiritual traditions, myths, gods, and goddesses represent this inner journey. They serve as external representations of what is within us and not as anything separate and apart from us—they are reminders. Enlightenment is not a metaphysical event—it does not happen outside the body but rather the key lies within the brain and nervous system. Spiritual awakening need not be relegated to only those who can withdraw from the world and devote all their time and effort to the spiritual life. Spiritual awakening is indeed a mystical science and can be understood and facilitated through information modern science is beginning to corroborate and uncover.

The inner-light perception referred to in the last couple of sutras is mentioned many, many times in the various spiritual literature of the world. So much so that the deeper meaning is often lost or overlooked. We take for granted the references to the "light within" as just flowery and poetic symbolism. Such descriptions for the most part are spoken of as if the light is purely symbolic.

However, in this context the real meaning and identity of the light is not symbolic—the light perceived within during surrendered meditation and moments of spiritual experience is the concrete "form" of the Divine in expression and not different or separate from the divine Source. It is Divinity in the "form" of light, the essence of being. The "light" is the background consciousness that is always present. Accompanying the light is the primordial sound—the sound and light are simply different aspects of the same thing. This sound is the steady hum of the vibration of manifest creation. It is behind all sound, perceived internally as the sound *Om*.

Some theorize that the experience and the perception of inner light occurs in the brain stem. This part of the brain is considered the most primitive—often called the "reptile" brain by modern science. However, yoga science offers a different perspective: consciousness enters the physical dimension through the brainstem and emerges into the physical plane to animate the body. At this level consciousness is pure and unmodified. But as pure consciousness filters up into progressively higher areas of the brain, it takes on the "impurities"—the characteristics and the corresponding mental modifications inherent to those areas. The light is the luminous nature of pure consciousness. However, as it moves away from the source, it is colored by the definitions that are the content of our brain's programming. We become identified by, and with, those contents. In effect, "the one becomes the many." We then falsely perceive ourselves as being defined by the contents rather than by our true identity as the light, the Self, pure consciousness.

The cells in this part of the brain stem have projections that ascend up into the brain and descend down the spine. The ascending tracts reach up encompassing the entire brain. Neuroscientists define areas in this lower part of the brain purely as an activating source and is why it is called the reticular (meaning net-like) activating system (RAS). It is thought to produce arousal and consciousness. As a subconscious scanner it looks for things in the environment that require the activation of the brain. These include things that are unique, familiar, or problematic. Why?

Because from an instinctive and survival perspective our brain is programmed to pay attention to these types of triggers. Otherwise, for the most part, we remain in autopilot, not requiring the energy expenditure and the need to be more aware. When the brain is in autopilot there is a predominance of electrical activity in the EEG called alpha rhythm, the brains "idle" frequency. The RAS finds no need to waste energy, so the cortex is in a relatively neutral state. However, as soon as something is perceived as "unique, familiar, or problematic," the RAS sends activating electrical signals to the cortex to *pay attention!* In those moments we are more "awake" as the brain is producing faster brain-wave activity called beta in preparation for appropriate action.

The brain waves themselves are tiny electrical pulses of light moving along intricate networks in the brain. The RAS is the pacemaker of the brain waves, and virtually all the electrical activity registered in the higher brain is turned on and off by this system. Brain death occurs when the RAS stops sending the signals and all electrical activity eventually ceases. This does not happen all at once but is a process that occurs within minutes after cardiac arrest.

A recent experiment intended to measure the EEG (brain waves) of the rat brain after cardiac arrest caught neuroscientists by surprise. The findings are detailed in a *National Geographic* article, "In Dying Brains, Signs of Heightened Consciousness." This information is providing a different perspective on what is happening in the brain during the dying process. Scientists are being extremely cautious about how to interpret this and the implications. This information potentially opens the door to understanding how the brain is involved in the mystical experience as well, since the brainwave activity has similar characteristics.

Some neuroscientists argue that the light phenomena that is perceived within, during the near- death experience (NDE) and in deep meditation, is just the effect of chemical changes, oxygen deprivation, and other mechanisms occurring in the brain. They tend to disregard the profound spiritual changes many who have NDEs have, as well as the profound spiritual experiences reported by beginning and advanced meditators alike as this inner light is perceived.

Many mystical teachings state that the light perceived within is the source of all living beings—it is our mutual home. It is the common core experience shared no matter the race, religion, or belief system. It is the profound meaning of the often spoken phrase "We are one." It is the well- spring of our deepest, innermost source of life. We can learn to perceive the light, immerse ourselves in the divine Consciousness therein, and meditate in it. Different cultural myths of sacred rivers, i.e. the Ganges, the Jordan, represent this sacred flow of life. We can learn to merge with and receive the inner revelation of Divinity and pure grace the light (the river) carries. The light within is divine Consciousness and will lead the individual to discover the depths of the Soul.

Reversing the Flow of Attention

Normally our awareness flows out to the external world. The nervous system has been trained to scan the external environment, to translate events as good, bad, or indifferent and to act accordingly. However, in order to perceive the inner light, attention must be redirected. This was discovered many thousands of years ago by spiritual adepts and is where many meditation traditions find their roots. There are ancient writings detailing the cranium, the spine, and other specific areas of brain anatomy as the "palatal house" with "doors" to the divine Consciousness. There are meditation techniques designed to access these areas within the brain and to reverse the "normally" outflowing consciousness driven by the RAS and redirect it back to the luminous source.

How to See the Inner Light and Hear the Inner Sound

Occasionally both beginning and advanced meditators spontaneously perceive the inner light during meditation sessions. Along with the light the sound *Om* is also often heard as well. Some do not see any light at all, just a field of darkness and specks of light, nor do they hear any sound in particular. However, there are techniques passed down from spiritual adepts that can enable the meditator to see the light and to hear the inner sound. In the kriya yoga tradition there is a light and sound meditation, using the sound *Om*, described below. This technique is one of the preliminary kriya yoga methods and with practice by itself will result in the inner perceptions. There are several additional stages to this technique that I will offer over time for those who are interested—stay tuned.

The Procedure

Sit in the ideal meditation posture: upright, firm but comfortable. Legs can be crossed or you can sit in a chair with your feet on the floor. If possible, sit with your back away from any support so that your spine is erect. Your chin should be pulled slightly in so the neck is not craned. You should feel as if there is a string pulling up the crown of your head toward the ceiling so your spine and neck are extended. Gently close your eyes. The room should be as quiet and dark as possible. If there is any light in the room then an eye mask can be useful. However, be sure the mask does not put any pressure on the eyeballs—pressure on the eyeballs will produce light phenomena in the eyes themselves. There is a product called iMask available on the internet and it is designed with a space between the eyes and the mask so there is no pressure on the eyes.

Earplugs can be used too to block out distracting sounds and to enable you to listen "within."

Sit for a few moments just to relax as you bring your attention to the natural and gentle rhythm of the breathing pattern—slow, gentle inhalation and slow gentle exhalation. The length of inhalation and exhalation should be approximately equal. This is natural breathing, no attempt to overly control the breath—just smooth, natural "belly" breathing.

After relaxing, when feeling calm and centered, bring your attention to the point at the center of the forehead between the eyebrows. This is known as the location of the "spiritual eye," in Sanskrit, Kutastha Chaitanya. This area also corresponds to the location of the brain's prefrontal cortex, the brain area associated with executive functions such as concentration, attention, planning, decision making, and impulse control. Do not cross or strain the eyes. Just gently lift the gaze as if looking at a slight angle up and out into the distance through the forehead. Imagine that the breath is moving in and out through this point.

When the breath is calm and quiet begin to mentally repeat the sound *Om* three times with inhalation and three times with exhalation. Feel or imagine that the sound *Om* is knocking at, or tapping, the spiritual eye point. Like this: as you inhale, *Om-Om-Om* and with exhalation, *Om- Om-Om*. Gently allowing the sound of *Om* to resonate and "tap" at the spiritual eye with each Om. Gradually and without discomfort, try to extend the number of *Om* repetitions up to six with inhalation and six with exhalation. As you do this look into the spiritual eye as if you are attempting to pierce it, as if looking through a veil to the other side. Try this as a meditation for at least ten minutes, longer if desired. Afterward, if you have another form of meditation that you use then just do that or whatever feels natural to you.

The light often appears in cloudy or misty shade at first with different colors flowing and melting into one another. The light is not actually being seen with the eyes but perceived in the "mind's" eye. Eventually as concentration improves certain specific colors and shapes related to different manifestations of consciousness begin to become more stable and clear. The mental repetition of the Om is gradually replaced by "hearing" the internal sound of *Om*. The sound of *Om* begins to arise along with the light and both become more distinct. The sound *Om* is actually a manifestation of the light and vice versa—they are the same. Many other sounds too may become noticeable but some of these can just be sounds of internal physiological processes in the body. Eventually, however, the sound of *Om* becomes quite clear, like a steady low frequency hum in the background. Some meditators report that even after meditation they perceive the sound *Om* when relaxed and in an environment that is quiet and relatively free of loud noises.

Both the light and the sound have a quality that becomes more and more tangible and recognized as the Divine Presence: a benevolent, gentle, uplifting, and assured sense of the omniscient presence of God within.

When the light and sound begin to come forward, the objective is to merge with the light and sound. Have the gentle intention to go beyond the initial perception and go through the light and sound to the origin. This is done by following the stream, as it were, looking and listening within, tracing back to the source.

> He who finds his happiness within, his joy within and likewise his Light within, realizes one-ness with the Divine and the beatitude of God.
> BHAGAVAD GITA 5:24

In the undistracted gaze Appears the Light
Gaze and gaze to heart's content And mingle one with it;
The Heavenly Stream will surge
To the spaces infinite of Void Space
Then may the Uncreated Being (pure consciousness) witnessed be.

                                                                             TIRUMANTIRAM, VERSE 600

Brain Sutra 25

"Liberation for Oneself and Service to Mankind."[7]

The culmination of life's lessons should result in the gradual peeling away of all attachments and all meaningless aims. Life is the great teacher and is leading us to the unfoldment and realization of our highest spiritual potential—liberation. On a daily basis we are bombarded with an entirely different definition of what success in life means. For many the mark of success is believed to be some form of ego "greatness" defined by illusory and transitory things. The media, marketing, and social influences portray varying degrees of obsession with ego drives: with the pursuit of wealth, power, pleasure, narcissism, youth, and beauty. There is nothing wrong with any of these drives if they serve as stepping stones and as a means to the final goal of liberation. We should have sufficient material support to fulfill our needs comfortably; we should be able to experience life's pleasures without undo sensation seeking; and we should fulfill our duty, called dharma, as it is presented to us. However, the danger lies in the unconscious attachment to transito-

---

7 "Liberation for oneself and service to mankind" is the motto of the Ramakrishna order of monks.

ry and illusory experiences and objects that only create more attachment and slow down our progress on the path.

No one belongs to you and you belong to no one. This is the ultimate truth and any notion of ownership or possession is illusion. We have a responsibility to all life and indeed we are stewards, but this role is often misunderstood. There are two forms of relationship to others: one unconditional, universal, and liberating, and the other conditional, personal, and stagnating. In Sanskrit they are known as *daya* and *maya*. Daya can be translated as compassion. Maya in this sense is attachment. When we are under the influence of maya our love is exclusive and conditional—it is relegated to our husband, wife, children, relatives, and then on a broader scale to our "tribe": friends, country, political party, religion, even our sports teams. With maya there is a notion of "I-me-mine" in how we relate to the world around us. My family, my wife/husband, my children, my money, my body, my country, my affiliation, my religion, my God! We have a sense of ownership and if we are not careful this becomes strong attachment.

The opposite of maya is daya. Daya is really a different-conscious perception; it is unconditional compassion for all life. It means looking upon everyone equally with the same eye of realization. Seeing all from the perspective of truth or Reality. We do not love anyone more or less in the highest form of love. There are great saints throughout history who have been observed to display profound compassion and love for all living things, including animals, plants and even inanimate forms. This is not just an attitude that we can hope for but is the essence of who we are. The saint is not "practicing" or blindly believing anything—the saint just happens to perceive through the awakened spiritual sense that one divine Being is manifesting as all things and playing all roles. This requires a detachment from the names and forms that appear as separate identities, as "others," and always acknowledging the true one Divine identity within.

Get Out of the Way!

The one divine Being, what religions give various names to, is manifesting as everything we see and is the essence of all Being. At the same time we cannot be naive in how we apply this truth. A story is told of a spiritual seeker walking down a path in the jungle. He saw a large elephant charging toward him! There was a rider on the elephant shouting, "Get out of the way!" But the seeker said to himself, "Well, all this is God, so I will just stand my ground in faith!" Shortly the elephant was upon him and picked him up with his trunk and tossed him aside. He was badly bruised and confused. When he came around to his senses he asked God, "What went wrong?" The reply was, "I am in everything, the elephant and the rider, and therefore I tried to warn you speaking as the rider to get out of the way!" There are times when we can stand our ground but as our intuition strengthens we will also know when to get out of the way.

Your Life Is a Parenthesis in Eternity

Our lives have been described as "a parenthesis in eternity." When we are young we feel immortal but as we age we perceive time as speeding up and we may begin to reevaluate our purpose for being here. So often we hear of people at the end of their lives having regrets over not paying more attention to spiritual values and truths. It is uncomfortable for most of us to contemplate the inevitability of departure from this life and the eventual separation from this relative plane of existence and from everyone we know. Our instinctive survival programming avoids this kind of thinking... and actually keeps us from confronting many things in our lives that we realize we should give attention to. It is easy to remain complacent and to ignore the passing of time, to avoid and to "put off until tomorrow." For many the concerns of family, finances, job, personal comforts, and personal health take the lead and become the primary focus of life. If any of this resonates with you, if you have any doubts, regrets, or anxieties, then now is the time to commit and to get your priorities in order. The number one priority is "liberation for oneself." Then and only then can we be of real service to mankind. All else follows and falls into place when we take the actions necessary and put our goal for liberation in its rightful place.

What Is Liberation?

Liberation is freedom from all that previously bound us and kept us from realizing the truth of our being—it is Self-realization. If we are embodied we are not yet fully liberated. To be accurate though, there are a very few who are liberated while embodied (called *jivan-muktas*) and their work on this plane has been accomplished. For these advanced Souls, final seed karmas are being worked out until they make their transition, not to return again if they so choose. The purpose of our embodiments is to achieve (or realize) liberation, and these lives are our school rooms. If we are not consciously living in the twenty-four-hour-a-day awareness of our Divinity and the Divinity in everyone and everything, then we are not yet liberated. Therefore, liberation is our number one priority.

How Do We Experience Liberation?

Liberation is our very nature as pure spirit but to realize our essence requires a path that incorporates spiritual disciplines. There are many paths. The truth is all paths lead to liberation sooner or later. Even what one would consider as "fundamentalist" paths and paths that clearly are suffering from distorted beliefs, will eventually lead one out of untruth to truth. How can this be? The answer is simple: every event and everything in our lives is conspiring to teach us.

Teaching can be gentle or severe but eventually actions and beliefs that contribute to suffering will be identified, realized, and corrected by every individual and his/her path will change or adjust accordingly. This can occur in this life or future lives but it will surely be a lesson repeated until it is learned. We must have utmost respect for all people no matter where they are in their unfoldment and no matter their chosen path, religion, or belief system; all will eventually reach the shore of liberation. If you have yet to find a clear path, open your mind and pray for guidance—it will be made clear. Know too that if you do not have a teacher or guru, the truth is, you already have one. The word *guru* means, "that which dispels the darkness." A real guru will tell the seeker that the true guru is not a person. Life is the guru. Life teaches the lessons that, by and by, dispel the darkness and ultimately lead every single Soul out of suffering and ignorance to final liberation.

All time is wasted that is not spent in seeking God.
LAHIRI MAHASAYA

Simplify, Simplify, Simplify

Life can be simplified and arranged so that we shift our time allotment from mundane matters to spiritual pursuits. First we devote some time every day to prayer, meditation, and to studying the nature of consciousness through spiritual literature and devotional practices. Eventually our spiritual senses begin to awaken. There is nothing wrong with socializing, cultural engagements or media entertainment, but we should be discreet and on guard as to what we let into our consciousness. Over time, as we progress, we will find that many of the mundane pursuits only provide temporary satisfaction, are a waste of time, and consequently lose their attraction. The satisfaction and pull of our unfolding Soul awareness begins to overwhelm all else. Over time, we will find that every spare moment is given to our spiritual disciplines, not because we "should" but because we realize that it is the single most important thing we can do, and the Soul satisfaction we experience as a result is beyond words. We arrange our lives around our spiritual disciplines rather than trying to "fit in the time." This does not mean that we have to become renunciates and isolate ourselves from the world and live like hermits. True renunciation is not an outer condition—it does not happen by avoiding, depriving, or taking things away. One can have nothing and be attached to everything. In truth, renunciation is internal and means we can *enjoy* all that comes to us but simply not be attached. We renounce our attachment to the things of this world so that we can find our real satisfaction within our Soul in communion with God.

The Promise

Over time the brain and nervous system will become more and more refined as we find the instinctive, distracting (and time-wasting) pleasure-seeking drives being replaced with a yearning for conscious Divine union. At a certain point we realize nothing else matters—there is an omniscient (all-knowing) presence that knows exactly how and what we need. Its intelligence is beyond our comprehension just as the infinity of the universe is beyond our intellect to grasp.

This Divine Presence is absolute existence and impersonal in the unmanifest aspect but is very personal and intimate in the manifest. The unmanifest is called the "Father" and the manifest is called the "Mother." Father is the transcendent, formless aspect and Mother is with form, immanent in creation. Therefore, one can experience the Divine manifest in creation easier than the unmanifest—and eventually the experience of the manifest leads to the experience of the unmanifest. Many saints call the manifest aspect the Divine Mother because of the creative, nurturing attribute one experiences when one communes with the Divine Mother—the universe and everything we perceive is the "body" of the Divine Mother. So even though we know we are one with absolute being (the formless transcendent aspect), having a sense of devotion and childlike relationship to the manifest expression of God as the Divine Mother can be very useful. Until we fully realize our oneness with the absolute transcendental being, we can access the Divine Mother presence through deep yearning. By using love as a magnet we attract that presence from within. God as the Mother aspect will respond to our pleas when we sincerely and continuously yearn to know his/her presence. Which in essence is love. Then it will arise within as an overpowering, yet tender and gentle, awareness. As described in previous sutras the presence is often unveiled in the meditator's spiritual eye in the form of light along with the sound of *Om*. We must be patient though; it may not be revealed right away. After pouring out our hearts we must learn to quiet our mind through meditation so we can look and listen within the depths of our being for the response. We must prepare the container also. The purity of body, mind and emotions is important. Purity of the body is facilitated by following a clean and appropriate diet—the Ayurvedic Sattvic diet is most supportive of this. For mental and emotional poise we can cultivate the virtues (reread Sutra 14) and work on any addictions or negative reaction patterns, thereby freeing ourselves of anger, greed, selfishness, pride, fear, egoism, and other impurities. This yearning must be from the Soul, very strong. Its intensity has been described as putting your head under water and yearning to breathe; more intense than the yearning the lover feels when their beloved is gone; more than the yearning a child feels for its missing mother! This is not an experience that only poets, saints, and mystics are privy to—this is our heart of hearts just waiting to be unveiled in the depths of the Soul.

In your quiet moments, pray to God, yearn to love God, yearn for knowledge and the love of God with the deepest devotion of your Soul—in time you shall receive the answer.

There is a candle in your heart, ready to be kindled.
There is a void in your Soul, ready to be filled.
You feel it, don't you? You feel the separation from the Beloved.
Invite Him to fill you up, embrace the fire.
Remind those who tell you otherwise that Love comes to you of its own accord,
and the yearning for it
cannot be learned in any school.

         RUMI ON YEARNING

Read less, meditate more, and think of God all the time.

         PARAMAHANSA YOGANANDA

Made in the USA
Middletown, DE
19 October 2022